GRACE

For The Contemplative Parent

By Lily Crowder

A Practical Guide For Mothers
Practicing the Presence of God

Sons of Thunder Ministries & Publications
Portland, Oregon

Grace For The Contemplative Parent by Lily Crowder

Published by:
Sons of Thunder Ministries & Publications
P.O. Box 40
Marylhurst, OR 97036

www.thenewmystics.com
Phone: 1-877-343-3245
Email: info@thenewmystics.org

Library of Congress Control Number: 2013913379
International Standard Book Number: 978-0-9770826-4-3

Printed in the United States of America

9 8 7 6 5 4 3 2 1

This book is dedicated to my husband John and my four children, Maile, Jonas, Nova and Ezekiel.

You are my favorite people and life's greatest teachers.

Contents

The Bible translations in this book can be identified by the following codes when used:

AMP – *The Amplified Bible* (Grand Rapids: Zondervan Publishing House and The Lockman Foundation, 1954, 1958, 1962, 1964, 1965, 1987). Translated mostly by Frances Siewert.
CJB – *Complete Jewish Bible* (Clarksville, MD: Jewish New Testament Publications, Inc., 1998). David Stern.
ESV – *The English Standard Version Bible: Containing the Old and New Testaments with Apocrypha* (Oxford: Oxford University Press, 2009).
KJV – *The Holy Bible King James Version: 1611 Edition.*
MOF – *The Bible: James Moffatt Translation* (San Francisco: Harper Collins, 1922/1994). James Moffatt.
NIV – *The Holy Bible, New International Version* (Grand Rapids: The Zondervan Corporation, 1973, 1978, 1984). International Bible Society.
NLT – *New Living Translation* (Wheaton: Tyndale House Publishers, 1996, 2004, 2007).

Preface
On Practicing His Presence

A few years ago I read *The Practice of the Presence of God* by Brother Lawrence, a devotional made from a compilation of letters and conversations from a 17th-century French monk. He had learned to practice the presence of God at all times, in every daily task and duty. His simple letters encourage readers to practice God's presence and see His glory in every facet of life. "He found that the shortest way to go straight to God was by a continual exercise of love and doing all things for His sake."[1]

Brother Lawrence purposed to engage in the Lord's presence during every hour of the day. He began to find an effortless, uninterrupted state of awareness and constant union with his Creator at every moment, unrestricted by whatever task was at hand. He also acknowledged that it is solely by God's grace that we can engage in this uninterrupted union with our Creator, giving no credit to works or deeds.

He wrote:

> *The time of work does not with me differ from the time of prayer. In the noise and clatter of my kitchen, while several persons are at the same time calling for different things, I possess God in as great a tranquility as if I were upon my knees at the Blessed Supper.*[2]

This was the concept he devoted himself to throughout his life, that wherever you are and whatever task is at hand, God's presence was to be known and practiced intentionally through His grace.

---

[1] Brother Lawrence, *The Practice of the Presence of God,* First Conversation.
[2] Ibid., Fourth Conversation.

Preface

I loved his writings and enjoyed the notion of this idea of *continual awareness,* but I was skeptical. Monastic living seemed to be a much more conducive lifestyle to engage in this type of uninterrupted awareness, than did mothering in the 21st century.

I wondered how did these ideas and experiences translate to my world, my sleep deprived, nursing, potty training, house cleaning, laundry folding, *can't even remember when I had my last uninterrupted moment of quietness,* phase of life?

I wanted the awareness of His presence and grace to transcend the noise and clutter in my life, and the peace Brother Lawrence spoke of to be consistent in my everyday duties of motherhood. I knew the Lord desired for me to find full pleasure in every moment, as unglamorous as any moment may have seemed. I began to take the practice of His presence into my world, finding pleasure in the awareness of His grace and the joy of His company, even while changing a dirty diaper. I remember thinking that one day I would like to write a devotional like *The Practice of the Presence of God,* only for mothers.

So here we are, my humble version of *Practicing His Presence* for parents ... most specifically for moms. This book is meant to be an encouragement for mothers to engage in a constant awareness (practice) of His presence in the daily, mundane tasks of motherhood. This book is a call to all mothers to feast on His grace; grace that invades every aspect of your home, your family and *you!*

This is not a *how-to* book on parenting! It is an awakening to a reality of Christ Who is already present in our homes.

I am aware of countless *how-to* books, and some are full of wisdom and grace. I have read and gleaned from many insightful, inspiring parenting books and articles, but I in no way cared or felt compelled to add to them; after all, I am still in the process of raising my four children. What wisdom would I have on the grandma of 11 grandchildren? I have so much more to learn! Everything I say in this book I will be saying again to myself as well.

I have been challenged, inspired, awe-struck and forever humbled by the call of motherhood; however, I could never begin or pretend to claim that I have an edge on any other parent around. If I can do this mommy thing, anyone can!

I have countless *matron mother heroes* I can look to for inspiration. These amazing women, of all ages, have given me examples and advice that I hope to pass on in my relationships with the next generation of mothers. I am so grateful that I do not have to *reinvent the wheel* in many areas of parenting because I am able learn from others' experience. What a gift!

I wish I had an easy *step-by-step manual to raising perfect children,* but that would take away all the mystery and adventure found in the parenting journey that reminds our hearts of the need for a constant ongoing relationship with our Father. Something so impossible, like the task of raising children, so perfectly highlights the need to be connected to a higher source. This book is simply an encouragement to parents to engage in Christ within us. I hope you are awakened to a mystical relationship with a living God who lovingly guides you day to day in the middle of the entire ruckus of life. *Practicing His presence* is vital in taking you from the duty of caring for small children with simple needs, like dirty diapers and boo-boos, to comforting the adolescent who is experiencing emotional emptiness and longings of the soul. The journey is so unpredictable and at times very tiresome. It is so easy to grow weary as a parent, but I hope you are encouraged and inspired by these words, to persevere in joy in light of who Christ is in you.

There is great joy and purpose in finding complete fulfillment in exactly what you are doing right now! Regardless of the season or circumstances, there is a consistent flow of grace available

Preface

to every one of us. There is a *happy place* found even in the midst of chaos.

Motherhood is awesome! I will be forever relentless in this claim.
It is my hope to see all mothers free from the false expectations and performances that religion places on women, and that out of this freedom in Christ, we will fully model the evidence of joy found in the grace God has given us. It is my hope, that because of our joy, motherhood will become an envied calling to the upcoming generation.

Enjoy your life! Enjoy your children! Enjoy your calling!

Lily Crowder

Chapter 1
The Practice of Being Loved
... and being a guilt-free parent

A lot of parents say that you make most of your parenting mistakes with your first child.

As I look back at the last 15 years of my oldest daughter's life, I can't help but wonder if that statement is at least partially true.

For me, from the onset of becoming a parent, I did it all wrong. Anything that could be done to cause me to feel guilty about poor parenting was probably accomplished in those first couple years of my daughter's life. I felt so guilty so many times about my poor choices or different mistakes as a new mom.

So many of us have struggled with feeling guilty over how we acted towards our children. It is a terrible feeling. Guilt robs us of so much! Our peace, joy and freedom can suffer under this self-condemnation. I want to share with you about how I struggled with guilt. More importantly, I want to share with you what delivered me from it.

I will tell my story without spilling out every little detail. I will only share what is needed to encourage other parents who may find themselves weighed down by feelings of inadequacy and self-reproach regarding their parenting skills. I believe a large part of this story isn't only mine to tell. It is always good to remember that our feelings and perception of ourselves are not always how we are viewed or perceived by our Father.

I grew up knowing the Lord in a Christian home – a very broken, dysfunctional Christian home – but I was still raised with the knowledge of Christ. I was your typical *Christian girl gone bad.* After a series of sad events and foolish choices in my life, I turned away from my faith and was basically *plain ol' naughty!* The unwise choices I kept making and the harmful people I kept migrating toward left me in a state of depression and emptiness. I knew enough of what was right and godly, but I refused to live in such a way. I hated myself for that. My struggle with identity and feelings of unworthiness made me hungry for healthy affirmation and affection. I was your classic *looking for love in all the wrong places* kind of girl. It wasn't too long before I ended up becoming pregnant at age eighteen.

I had to humbly face my old Christian community and small town friends, move in with my mom and live off welfare. It was such a lonely, humiliating time in my life. Being *knocked up* and abandoned by someone who had claimed to care for me was overwhelmingly heartbreaking and humbling to say the least. If I hadn't had my dear mom around, and friends who loved me, I don't know what I would have done.

For the duration of my pregnancy I focused on trying to get my life back together. I had a desperate hunger to make up for all the wrong I had done. I felt so undeserving of anything good. I remember thinking that I was going to be punished for all my sin, and God was going to give me a horribly challenging baby. I felt so alone, undeserving and scared.

When my labor finally came on, I had no clue what was about to take place. I could only anticipate an outcome from a place of fear, rejection and uncertainty. But in that fragile place, when I was in labor, I could feel and sense the love and gentleness of Jesus. That day changed my life forever.

After a very long labor I gave birth to a beautiful, healthy baby girl. She was perfect, just perfect! The love for her that freely came from deep within me was overwhelming and unexpected. I didn't even know this kind of love for another person existed. I had no words or definition, and still have none, to describe my experience. She was amazing – such perfection, such tiny wonder. I could not believe she was my daughter. In those first moments with her I couldn't help thanking and praising the Lord for her life. There seems to be nothing in this life that can draw

Chapter 1

such awe and praise out of even the most fearful heart than bringing a child into the world. The moment when a mother sees her baby for the first time face-to-face transcends all time and space. That moment seemed *other-worldly* to me. I named her Maile (*My-lee,* which is Hawaiian for *beautiful)* Joy. I couldn't help but feel that I didn't deserve this! What about my punishment? I did everything wrong and yet here I was holding this beautiful, perfect baby girl – a perfect gift.

Every day she got cuter. She had two huge dimples when she smiled and glorious, perfect baby rolls. She was so happy! Because of her happy nature she was soon dubbed *the cutest and easiest baby anyone had ever met.* And she really was! To this day, we still call her *Smiley Maile!*

As a new mom, I could feel God's grace and His presence, mostly in the way that He provided a natural, new love and inspiration in me for my daughter. Having a sweet, innocent person to love and nurture gave me purpose and a renewed sense of self, even during the really lonely moments. When all my friends were out on the town and I was home alone with my baby and my dog, a sweet chocolate Labrador named *Matty,* I knew God had a plan and that my daughter was one of the best parts of it. I really enjoyed being a mom, even a single mom, to my adorable baby girl. Maile and I would do everything together. God provided a job as a nanny where I was able to take my daughter to work with me. Because of her wonderful demeanor, I was even able to take her to my college classes. I look back at pictures of my daughter and me back then, and we were always doing something fun like hiking, camping, playing in the mountains or at the beach. We were so happy together. But at times, when I was still, I would think of her future and the reality of being a young single mom; I felt guilty. I felt guilty for the lack of a father and guilty for all my inabilities to provide everything I thought she needed. Those feelings were paralyzing at times.

Chapter 1

When Maile was two I met my husband, John. I was at a place in my life where I felt really committed to the Lord. I had moved to Homer, Alaska, and I was plugged in with an awesome church community. I was content in raising my daughter in Alaska and convinced it would be years before I could ever feel worthy enough to get married. I wasn't even looking. Then just one day after I turned 22, who should show up in Alaska? All the way from Georgia came this tall, dark, handsome and wonderfully witty John Crowder. He had a ponytail back in those days, and I used to wear homemade patchwork hippy clothes. I am six feet tall and he is six foot five inches – that was good enough for me!

I could barely stand when I first spoke to him, nor could he! Something in me knew that He was *the one* from the very first day I met him, so much so that I tried to hide from him in the basement of the church where we met! It was so obvious to everyone around us that there was a little more than chemistry going on between us. You could almost hear Barry White music playing whenever we were around each other. It was love – for the first time in my life, real love. It was completely supernatural! Falling in love with John was the best time in my life. I have this keen, elephant-like remembrance of all our first moments of that first summer we spent together charted out in my memory. I could tell you every outfit John wore, every place we went, what we ate, what we said and all the days and times everything took place. A day felt like a week and weeks felt like years, so it is no surprise that we were married five months after we met!

Along with meeting and falling in love with me, John also fell in love with my little blue-eyed girl. I have a letter John wrote to me after we were engaged, while he was away working on a fishing boat on the Bering Sea. The letter was a beautiful confession of what was taking place in his heart for my little girl. The idea of being her father was effortless and natural, like it had always been part of the plan. When he had first met me, he knew he would marry me. And when a little girl came and held my hand, he knew she was going to be his daughter. John adopted Maile shortly after we were married. She was three and grew to know and trust him like he had been there from the very first day. Maile became, and still is until this day, *Daddy's girl.* The bond and connection that my daughter and her dad share is amazing to see.

My story of early motherhood and becoming a wife is full of God's redemptive sovereignty. I wouldn't trade this transformation, my story, for anything, even with all the awkward, hard moments involved. God's love unexpectedly burst into my life and made things new. I could not have known such love unless I was shown it; *we love because He first loved us.* There is such wealth in experiencing great love and redemption in any area of our life. To this day, I still remember what it was like to feel like an outsider. When I see another young girl or single mom struggling, I am able to encourage her by sharing my story.

I remember a time when my daughter was about two, before I had met John, I was alone in my little Alaskan cabin. I opened my Bible for the first time in a long while to the scripture, "Therefore, I tell you, her many sins have been forgiven – as her great love has shown. But whoever has been forgiven little loves little" (Luke 7:47, NIV). I knew God was going to cause me to love much because I had been forgiven much.

God gave me a loving husband, and He gave Maile a loving dad. But for some reason, I still felt like more penance for all my sin was due. I felt guilty for the days ahead when I would have to share with my daughter the truth about her adoption. I even felt guilty for making John take care of us! It was a crazy lie I believed. At that time in my life, I had little understanding of the cross in its entirety. I didn't understand how it transforms our imperfect lives completely by the free gift of His death.

On one hand, my imperfect and non-ideal introduction to parenting gave me a perspective of necessary need for God's

Chapter 1

grace. But on the other hand, when I began to feel more *together* and in control of my life, I felt a need to arm myself with inner healing tools and self-help books to make sure the harmful effects of my past sins wouldn't creep back up and ruin my life or my children's lives.

This is how guilt works ... just when we are enjoying the fruit of a free gift that we didn't deserve or have to work for, religion tries to con us into thinking we will need to work to maintain such a good thing. Religion will always make you *work* for a *free* gift. Religion will make you feel guilty because you can never do enough. You will never get it all right by yourself. It is futile.

My past was just an isolated, bigger reason that contributed to my anxiety and guilt about my parenting. I have felt guilty for countless reasons over the years. There always seems to be some area that I *miss it!* Let's face it; parenting is some tough stuff to handle on our own. The pressure to acquire all the skills and master all the techniques necessary in raising each of our very different children, in a way that ensures they will not be hurt or harmed, is no small mountain to climb. No parent knows what the heck he or she has gotten into when a newborn comes home – unpredictability becomes the norm. When you have a baby you are in the trenches, folks! It feels like trying to thread a needle on the back of a mountain goat scaling the Himalayas. We are trying to keep up with all the unique emotional, physical and spiritual needs our little dependents require in order to mature into healthy functional adults. All this while trying to scrapbook, lose weight, keep up with the dusting, pay the bills, read the emails and then still have energy for your husband when nighttime rolls around! There is always going to be at least one day you feel totally defeated and inadequate at your job. Then there will be those days when you just feel totally inadequate.

We don't just feel guilty about the big things; we feel guilty about little things as well: *I yelled too loud. I let them watch a potentially spirit-harming movie. I fed them popcorn and ice cream for dinner. They all have cavities. I was too busy to listen, too tired to talk. I don't read to them enough. I let my child be with someone that may have hurt him or her.* The list is endless. I have even felt guilty for the mistakes *our* parents have made and how they may affect their grandchildren. It never ends!

His cross is a guilt-free feast!

When we entertain feelings of guilt, we are inclined to parent out of a place of insecurity. When we are motivated to parent out of guilt and insecurity, then we rob our home of a security that comes from trusting that everything is okay and our shortcomings are forgiven. Guilt is not our portion as believing parents! We are forgiven for every time we have blown it. To remain guilty is such a waste of energy and time. We have to let it go!

He came to abolish sin and its harmful effects forever! His death on the cross was a free antidote for something we could never and will never be able to fix.

Guilt comes to invade and rob our relationships. His Grace enables our relationships to emulate true love, health and freedom.

Guilt perverts how we love. His Grace allows pure love to flow from us.

Guilt blocks us from receiving love from others. Grace opens us up to receive love fearlessly.

Entertain the effects of His forgiveness in your home; meditate on it at the end of a bad day. Don't let the guilty effects of sin contradict the power of the cross in your family.

When I really heard the Gospel in a way that highlighted our complete forgiveness and wholeness in Christ, and when I began to believe I was fully forgiven and made new through His grace, then I was able to let go of guilt. I was able to focus on the greatness of His love, rather than the inadequacy of my performance. There was a joy that replaced sorrow and mourning over my past mistakes or my present failures. I began to have such confidence and peace. The effects of mom believing that Christ has made all things new and whole were noticeable not just to myself, but to my children and husband.

His blood applies to every aspect of our lives, including me getting knocked up as a teenager 15 years ago, or me yelling at my preschooler 15 minutes ago. Grace replaces something we would otherwise feel guilty and condemned about and gives us freedom instead. It infuses us with an identity of wholeness that liberates us from making those mistakes again.

It is good when Holy Spirit corrects us. When we are challenged about an area in our parenting that we need to *fine-tune*, we should embrace direction. George Eliot said, "It is never too late to be what we might have been." It is never too late to say sorry or to make amends for hurtful things you may have said or done. It is never too late to break a bad habit or enforce a new good habit in your home. It is never too late to be the mother who you know you really are in God's eyes. Remember, it is His kindness that highlights and brings correction, not condemnation. Grace comes in and teaches, influences and empowers our homes. We become pro-active, motivated parents through love, not guilt.

Parents are great candidates for the Gospel
We may make many mistakes at parenting. But failure is not inevitable! This is why a parent makes such a great candidate for the Gospel. Being faced with something as unpredictable and challenging as parenting is such a great opportunity for God to show off! He wants to show you how sweet His mercy is, how deep His wisdom is, how endless His love is and how sufficient His grace. Parenting is a perfect place for us to take notice of a good God, even in our weakness. Where we have been tempted to give our shortcomings and failures

Chapter 1

precedence over what He has done through Christ, we can now rest and enjoy a greater truth.

Without a Gospel lens, parenting is the hardest, most drawn-out job ever! Anyone that told you it was all *babies' breath* and *cuddly munchkin love* was full of it. It is the most challenging thing I know. Parenting paints a real definition of perseverance – hard-core perseverance! Just when I think I figured out each one of my kids, and I have this mom thing under control, some kind of dynamic rapidly changes. Our kids are always changing; their needs are always changing. Parenting is such a great way to trick us into giving up. God loves it when we give up. He has been waiting for us to give up and let Him take over with His grace all along.

Give up! Don't waste any more time feeling guilty, moms and dads. Replace those minutes, days and years you've spent wallowing in guilt and spend them fearlessly loving the people around you. There is no sin or mistake that is not reconcilable. He has forgiven you. His forgiveness is endless – limitless. Knowing this will set you free.

The Christian does not think God will love us because we are good, but that God will make us good because He loves us. – C.S Lewis

The Practice of Bein___
... and knowing you are not missing __

I think I was about five years old when I first imagined myself being a mom. It wasn't just a game of playing with a doll and pretending I was its mother – I imagined being the real kind of mom, nursing, changing diapers, caring for a home, holding and loving little ones. I remember being at a lake near our home in Idaho and watching two ducks and a trail of little ducklings following close behind. Everything about that picture seemed right; it seemed natural to see a family of ducks moving carelessly along in a swirly rhythmic paddle. That lake would have felt so empty and boring without that sweet duck family as its inhabitants. Something in me knew that would be my life one day, not as a duck family of course, but I just knew that one day I would be a wife and a mom with a trail of sweet *ducklings* in tow. At that moment, all I wanted to be was a mother. It felt so satisfying to have motherhood at the forefront of my goals and aspirations as a young girl. I knew undoubtedly what I was called to be. Motherhood beckoned me with untainted romance. Motherhood was a beautiful poetic picture of happy duck partners on a serene pond with happy ducklings following all in a perfect line. Motherhood felt right. It felt natural.

Important Mom
By the time I turned 27 I had four children. I didn't have time to even think or plan out children; I just did it, so to speak. Shortly after my youngest was born, John's first book, *The New Mystics,* was published. Almost overnight, as John's book quickly circulated, our simple little family, living a simple life in a small Alaskan town, was launched into a full-time international ministry. The adjustment to life in the spotlight and on the road as a family was stretching and growth-provoking to say the least. From the onset we purposed to make ministry a *family thing*, rather than just *Dad's thing*. We saw the importance of doing what it took to be together and support John's calling. I

Chapter 2

..s confident in what John was called to do, and his calling
became my calling as part of the Crowder family unit. This
meant leaving a safe predictable routine of life at home and
embracing the constant unpredictability of life on the road. It
also meant many grueling hours in the car. We did home
school, Easter and birthdays in hotels. We met best friends and
said goodbye all too quickly.

Our years of traveling as a family have given us countless
memories and fun stories. My children have been to all 50
states, and I have lost count of all the countries. There were
moments when we would have major meltdowns, especially
me, but overall the experience has been so great and so
enriching for each of us. I never pictured doing motherhood on
the road, even though I have always been adventurous. But I
am so thankful to have remained a family team as my husband
was sent out.

In the early years of ministry, especially when my children were
so little, John would do all the public speaking. I was focused
on entertaining my children and connecting with other mothers
at the numerous places we visited. I remember being
approached by countless empathetic individuals, many who
had observed me caring for my four young children while John
ministered in the spotlight. A few people would feel a need to
encourage me in light of my present situation as a full-time
mother. In their eyes I was missing all the fun, having to hang in
the back with my babies playing with Legos and reading board
books to my toddler.

"Lily, one day you will be called into a great ministry, and you
will be used mightily," they would say.

One day? The *one day* they referred to was not in reference to
my present season. It was far off, after I wasted the current
years toiling in the mundane, unglamorous duties of
motherhood *(note sarcasm)*.

Chapter 2

I remember feeling the need to apply myself to something more *productive* in addition to my daily duties. I would think, *"Maybe I should pull away to focus on my ministry."* I noticed all the women speakers and worship leaders, and I couldn't help but feel a little envious.

In some ways I felt obligated to prepare myself for my preacher-lady début, to position myself for the launching of my ministry. Maybe John would stay home so I could tour around the globe impacting the nations? Maybe I could wear a *she-suit* and get regular facials, or take the minimalistic poverty role of the missionary who lives amongst the poor in India. Then I would really be impacting the world for the Gospel! I would go home and pour into scriptures taking notes with anticipation that at any moment my *great ministry* would bloom.

In reality, I was never naturally inclined to ambitiously pursue a ministry or career outside my family; I was simply responding out of obligation and because of external pressure. Let's face it, being in the nursery doesn't come at the top of our *most glamorous things to do in the church scene* list. My new ministry never bloomed. I stayed with my true calling, mothering my four children. I focused on planning the next healthy meal, making sure the laundry was clean, teeth were brushed, favorite stories were read and songs were sung. Motherhood filled every seam and stitch of my time, and to be honest, I loved it!

I know it sounds silly and distorted, but I remember feeling a bit guilty for not pursuing what was perceived as *great* and *recognizable.* As if I could be hiding from my calling behind my children, slowly dying to my destiny in apathy masked as motherly responsibilities. But I wasn't apathetic! I didn't feel called to do anything greater than mother my children, stand by my husband and take care of our home. This is my calling. This is my most valuable use of time; maybe not forever, but definitely for now! There is truth in the good ol' clichéd phrase we have heard other woman say, *Your children are your ministry.* My children are my ministry! They are a full-time calling, and I am happy to spend myself on them. They are a ministry that is already in full bloom. I do not have to wait for a momentum to build or a platform to be established. The ministry of motherhood was up and running the minute I said, "I am pregnant!"

I am happy to stay home with my babes. I am happy to stand in the back with them at any church meeting. I am happy to put all my plans on hold when they get sick or if they have a dance recital. I am a mother. This is what I do. This is what I love. It is natural and a beautiful calling.

With all that said, I would also like to add that I know and admire some amazing woman with small children who are called to speak around the world, lead worship or work a full-time job. There is a real anointing and grace on them to go when and where they are needed. They are backed and supported by their husbands, and their children's needs come first. To see this transpire is amazing and inspiring! I don't criticize or judge any woman for pursuing a calling alongside raising her children.

I also know the wonderful people who encouraged me to look for *a more fulfilling career* meant only the best for me. But if the main job or calling for you in this season is at home raising a family – it's an amazing joy! What a privilege. Don't wait for someone to recognize what a blessed calling it is before you value what you do. You really aren't missing out on anything!

Wishing time away
When I was younger, before I had children, I loved to backpack. I craved trekking off into isolated, raw beauty. I was so mesmerized with the idea of being miles away from civilization. I know it isn't every young girl's passion, but I loved all the elements of a good backpacking trip: breathing fresh air, climbing challenging mountains, taking in views and enjoying silence for whole days at a time. This was my favorite form of recreation. But sometimes, during my excursions, I found

myself constantly thinking about where I wanted to hike next, worrying about the logistics of the next backpacking trip. All my thoughts and mental energy were directed towards another journey, not the one I was presently on. It was almost like I couldn't enjoy where I was at the moment, not completely, because I was focused on getting to the next trail in the next place. The glimpses of beauty and the satisfaction of a long climb felt so fleeting at the thought of all the other trails and adventures that I had not yet been able to complete. What was supposed to be a meditative, amazing, and an all-encompassing adventure seemed exasperating and unsatisfying.

Now, as a mother, I can compare my experiences with my children to a backpacking trip. Except now I am carrying four people's packs and not just my own. It is an adventurous journey to say the least! At times there is a temptation to long to be somewhere else and hurry up and get this trip over with. Sometimes I am lured by a thought or idea that tries to pull me away from the joy and beauty of the calling of motherhood. So many moms can be caught in a place of wonder lust, lured by an idea that there may be a better way to spend our time. We can *miss the diamond while chasing sparkles* when we are lured away from our season of motherhood. You may not have much encouragement in what you are doing every day, but the pleasure of the Lord is so vibrant when you serve your family. I am so thankful for the gentleness of Holy Spirit Who keeps reminding me, *Lily, you are not missing one thing!* Meditating on this truth allows me to find freedom to just enjoy where I am and what I am doing.

Every time I found out I was pregnant, I honestly would be so overwhelmed just thinking about the responsibility of another little dependent life growing inside of me. Sometimes I would lay in my bed and cry for about two days. I know that sounds really sad, but I would really be so overloaded with emotions (and hormones) and crying seemed like the best idea at the time. Was that selfish? *Yes!* We have all been selfish in some way. We all were designed as unique individuals – but our rugged independence is not the true source of joy. Of course it is healthy to have a sense of privacy and personal space. Everyone knows that when you have a baby, all that *personal space* gets 100 percent invaded. Parenting is a big responsibility, probably the only thing besides being married that really teaches us to live selflessly. A mother can really understand the concept of *laying down one's life.*

With each pregnancy I would surrender to some unappealing facts—a lot of unappealing facts. Yes, I would have to get fat again, and just when I had finally lost all my previous baby weight. Yes, I would be pushing a rather large Crowder kid out of a rather small area of my body (and the amount of pain that entails could not be summed up properly within my limited English vocabulary). Yes, I would have to nurse again, which meant being covered in milky fluid for at least a year – not ever being able to wear the clothes I wanted because they were not conducive to nursing. I would be changing diapers, giving baths and living a life not at all accommodating to all the grown-up stuff I wanted to do. Oh, and let's not forget sleep! Sleep becomes a new mom's most precious commodity. After I had my first baby, for my birthday, the only thing I asked for was for someone to take my baby so I could sleep the whole day!

Now that it has been many years since my last birth, and I have not nursed for a long while, I have found myself in a place in life where I am more free to do *big people stuff.* I look back at my pregnant and nursing phase, and I miss it so much! I miss the newborn smell. I miss the sound of a nursing baby and the way they look up at you when they are so full and content on milk. I miss the funny toddler years where you find your little one in the craziest mischief. I remember finding one of my toddlers in the sink with scissors, her hair cut to the scalp, but only on one side! At the time I think I was horrified, but now it is the funniest story. I wonder if I still had a nursing baby and a toddler running around with a comical haircut, would I still feel as romantically sappy about my life? Probably not, or maybe only when the kids were asleep and I had enough time after an intensely busy day to pause and watch them dream. Even now that my babies are big, sometimes after they are asleep, I want to wake them up just to tell them how precious they are and how sorry I am for being so busy and stressed that day to notice. As I look back at that season of little nursing babies and toddlers, I remember those years as some of the sweetest times of my life, even though I can freely admit they were chaotic and wildly busy.

Now I am busy in a different way. I have evolved into the unofficial role of *Taxi Mom*. I spend hours and hours each week shuttling kids to lessons and school. I still manage the home and attempt to meet the needs of all four of our kids in their new phases of life, as well as the needs of my husband. Everyone's needs have changed. The needs of crying toddlers, who could so easily be appeased with some goldfish crackers and a *Winnie the Pooh* video, have been replaced by the deeper emotional needs of teenagers: needs that I just cannot fill on my own. It really does not get any easier as our children get bigger. It just gets different. I often find myself in a fog, where I am too busy or tired to engage in what I am doing with my children. But I want to remember childhood is precious; it is fleeting, and I am not missing out on anything better than these kids. I pray I am always listening to my children when they have something to say. I pray I can capture every moment with them out of a place of pure gratitude.

Teach us to number our days aright, that we may gain a heart of wisdom (Psalm 90:12, NIV).

Teach us to realize the brevity of life, so that we may grow in wisdom (Psalm 90:12, NLT).

I find it humorous when I meet a young, single person that groans about how busy and tired they are. When they say, "I am so tired!" I think and want to say, *"Tired? Busy? Just wait until you're a mother! You see these dark circles under my eyes,*

Chapter 2

Honey? Do you realize I can't remember if I even brushed my teeth today?" But I don't say that of course. I remember not knowing the true definition of what it means to be really tired and really busy. What I wouldn't give to have that kind of free time again, but with the knowledge I have gained from having children. However, it doesn't seem to work that way.

Every aging individual realizes at some point in their rapidly changing life that time is very, very short. What has passed in our youth, and was not enjoyed, seems so valuable and priceless in hindsight.

I have met older moms, with children all grown and off living their lives, who recite the old cliché, "Enjoy those babies, because they grow too fast!" Those women are right! I laugh at how I have now become the imploring mother. Whenever I meet a stressed out new mama I tell her the same thing, "It goes by fast, enjoy every minute!"

I have had many epiphanies over the preciousness of time as a mother. Nothing seems to highlight the valuable commodity of time and the shortness of this life as watching our kids grow. Every milestone marks a passing moment that can never be repeated. Your newborn, who initially robs you of much needed sleep and leaves you wondering if he or she will ever grow past the challenging phase, finally sleeps through the night. Then your little night owl suddenly crawls, then walks, grows teeth and utters his or her first words! Your baby, who is no longer a baby, starts kindergarten, takes the training wheels off the bicycle, learns to read, loses teeth, starts driving, becomes a fully independent adult and gets married! I have not seen all my kids reach *all* these phases yet, but I know they are coming fast and are going to happen much sooner than I would like.

Every phase happens differently for each of our children. But these phases do come and go, in and out like the tide. Every changing moment is a beautiful reminder to be present in this minute, hour, day and year, as well as a reminder to number our days rightly. What a gift we have been given in watching our children transition from phase to phase. These big and little milestones, like losing teeth, become simple gifts that highlight life and all its sweetness.

I have all my children's front teeth collected in my jewelry box – hopefully cavity free! It hit me hard when my youngest lost his front teeth. He was the last six-year-old of my tribe of four to lose his front teeth! I wanted to take those teeth and mount them on the wall for the entire world to see. Those little teeth would shout, "LIFE IS SHORT! ENJOY IT!" Enjoy the littleness, and the bigness, and all that is in between.

I know I am not supposed to wallow in ridiculous sentimental moments of the days and times gone by. Weeping over memories that I cannot relive is pretty much a waste of time. That is not the point of these milestone reminders. I have been given these milestones to highlight how valuable every second is, and to embrace all of life with gratitude. It isn't time spent wallowing in bittersweet memories that produces fruitful, meaningful ways to spend our next hours and days. Rather it is Wisdom that highlights what is important and truly priceless.

En-joy: to take pleasure or satisfaction in
(Merriam-Webster Dictionary)

We all want to find contentment, rest and the freedom to enjoy where we are. We are looking for a quality that supersedes the quantity of our schedules, a satisfaction and pleasure in our daily routine. We want more than going through the motions, checking out and pushing our *autopilot* button.

Our lives are meant and designed by our Creator to be heightened by His presence in whatever we are doing, big or little. The awakening to God in everything and everywhere is our spring of life, our Technicolor reality in what once seemed dull

Chapter 2

and grey. We are not meant to be *zombie moms* seemingly lifeless and weighed down by obligation. We are called to be aware of our union with Christ and the fullness of the life we have in Him. God has called us all, even us moms, to enter into the enjoyment of being a parent. There is such a satisfaction in realizing the gift we have in being a mom!

When we are aware of the existing presence of God in our lives, we begin to notice a tangible joy in the seemingly mundane. The perspective of His Grace takes us from one of daily drudgery, to complete enjoyment in all aspects of being mom. That is the place where we can really sit back and be content in this calling.

With this fresh understanding you become alive to all aspects of this journey called motherhood. The infrequent rejuvenating moments of alone time, and the exhausting tasks can both be enjoyed. It is so easy to take this life for granted. It is also so easy to feel *taken for granted!* It is also all right to have other aspirations. You are free to dream about your next adventures and ambitions, even goals and pursuits that don't involve your children, without dismissing the value of where you are right now. I dream about going back to school to study art one day, but for now I am content to go paint once a week alongside my children. Regardless of the approval of others, our feelings or emotions or our personal aspirations, God has made a way for us to find pleasure in what we do every day. When the truth and value of your calling as a mother is highlighted, through Holy Spirit, you will never be able to take another moment for granted.

There are so many things I would like to do. I would love to travel more with my husband, get in really great shape, read more books and volunteer more in our community. At times I can feel torn and pulled in so many directions. It can feel defeating not being able to pour yourself into one thing fully, and having to do so many things *half-assed*. I can't begin to tell you how many unfinished projects are lying around my house.

Chapter 2

We refer to these projects as UFOs, un-finished objects/obstacles. But in the middle of all of those bits and pieces I remember that I can only do one thing really, really well. I can't do all things and be in all places at once. So if I have to choose just one thing to do really well, for now it is going to be raising my kids. That is something I know I will never regret.

We can be honest and admit parenting is challenging and chaotic. But there is beauty hidden in that chaos, and you always have an opportunity to find it if you so choose.

Don't let religion or society distract you!

One never has to look far to see that being a mother doesn't rank number one as an ideal goal amongst the people of our culture. Kids seem to be portrayed as inconvenient in so many subtle ways in our society. People are getting dogs instead of becoming parents. Even a recent Starbucks coffee cup quoted, "Dogs are the new kids." It is our job, as Christian families, to paint a picture of the true beauty of the family again. Society is craving healthy families, even if they do not know it.

Even some of the young girls I meet in the church have mentioned a desire to put motherhood way off for now. These young girls would rather travel or pursue a career. I think some of these girls and young women have seen the role of motherhood portrayed as a rather oppressive obligation because of the religious expectations put on mothers by the church body. I cannot blame them for being turned off at the thought of being a frumpy, lonely church mom. I have personally felt some of those religious expectations, making raising a young family seem more like a *dead work,* rather than a gift to enjoy.

I have known a few families so focused on child rearing techniques and discipline, hoping to have the best-behaved kids in church, that the whole family seemed tense and miserable. I wonder if those parents ever enjoyed their children

31

in the process of creating a military-style home. I also remember all the books I was encouraged to read as a new mom like, *How to be a Proverbs 31 Woman.* We would read these books in my church groups and discuss what was considered proper protocol for every facet of parenting. Through a lot of trial and error, I quickly learned that a lot of these *good ideas* were not necessarily the Lord's protocol, but rather the protocol of particular church groups and trends. I think back to some of the things I said or did out of religious obligation, and those thoughts send chills down my spine. How good it feels to be free from all that crap!

Anything that takes a gift and turns it into a work is religion.
– John Crowder

Don't let religion burden and weigh you down, moms! Don't feel obligated to find new things to do and work for to obtain parental success. It has been my experience that when I am motivated to parent, discipline and train my children out of joy and freedom, and not out of performance, I not only enjoy my kids more – but we also see more fruit in their character.

You are free to enjoy parenthood as a gift! Flaunt that gift to the world and to the next generation of women. Moms, remind our culture and the church how awesome it is to be a parent. Let the joy and freedom you walk in, as parents, be the envy of all who take notice.

Said the Eternal to Abram, "... I will make a great nation of you and bless you and make you famous for your bliss ... till all nations of the world seek bliss such as yours" (Gen. 12:1-3, MOF).

Chapter 3
The Practice of Awareness
... and seeing that God is everywhere

Where can I go from your Spirit? Where can I flee from your presence? If I go up to the heavens, you are there; if I make my bed in the depths, you are there. If I rise on the wings of the dawn, if I settle on the far side of the sea, even there your hand will guide me, your right hand will hold me fast. If I say, "surely the darkness will hide me and the light become night around me," even the darkness will not be dark to you; the night will shine like the day, for darkness is as light to you (Psalm 139:7-12, NIV).

There is nowhere we can go to escape Him. He has covered every square inch with His light. Even the darkness is as light to Him. What a comforting truth to share with a child who is scared at night.

Holy Spirit is not any less present in your munchkin packed minivan than He is in a church service. He is able to sneak and spill into every corner of our day – the grocery store, coffee shop, school and the work place. There is no place too dingy, dismal or seemingly unspiritual that He has left empty.

Reconnecting our focus to the reality of the presence of God in every place will change how we spend our lives. When we know just how connected to God we really are – not just in theory – when we really know how much He fills and consumes all the earth, our whole day changes. A day that feels like toil and a meaningless hamster wheel is transformed into one that contains purpose, full of meaning and substance. When you recognize Him in common places, you feel connected to Him personally. This is what He desires for us, to always feel united in our everyday lives.

Chapter 3

While the awareness of God's presence may seem highlighted in one particular environment or moment, the truth is, He has always been there! It is funny how we limit ourselves in our minds to recognizing Him. But I love it when He sneaks up and shows you that He has been there all along.

We have been going to a park by our house for the last four years. We have been there for every season: winter, spring, summer and fall. Recently we were visiting the park, walking down the same familiar path to the play structure, when we noticed another group of mothers and kids picking cherry plums from the trees that lined the path. I was amazed as I looked up in those trees and saw hundreds of delicious, perfectly ripened cherry plums all within arms reach! We had walked down that path all summer and three previous summers before, and never once noticed all this wonderful fruit just waiting to be picked. Now, every time we walk the path down to the park, the plum trees are the first things we notice. We observe the trees change with the seasons; the rich ruby red leaves in the fall, the extra sunlight on the path peering through leafless branches in the winter, the first sign of fruit buds in the spring, followed by ripe, juicy plums to enjoy at the end of the summer. We will wait expectantly for the end of this next summer to snack on them again!

We all have routines. I do the same thing pretty much every day. I get up, make my coffee and cook some breakfast for the kids. There is always a load of laundry to do, rooms to be cleaned and errands to be run. In your regular life, in your regular routine, just like that and by surprise you will notice Jesus has been there the entire time.

Brother Lawrence said, "The time of work does not with me differ from the time of prayer. In the noise and clatter of my kitchen, while several persons are at the same time calling for different things, I possess God in as great tranquility as if I were upon my knees at the Blessed Supper."[3]

Maybe you are not exactly "possessing God in great tranquility" in the middle of your routine. Maybe you just know He is there, and there seems to be a sense of rest in the middle of the busyness of your day. The confidence and rest that comes when we are suddenly graced with consciousness of His presence is so encouraging. It will become addicting and an instinctive desire will arise to recognize Christ everywhere. Practicing His presence will soon become a natural habit, and, as Brother Lawrence experienced, the difference between sensing God in a serene environment or activity will seem the same as sensing Him and enjoying Him in your messy kitchen with the kids screaming in the background.

Cultivating His Presence

Examine yourselves as to whether you are in the faith. Test yourselves. Do you not know yourselves that Jesus Christ is in you? Unless indeed you are disqualified. But I trust that you will know that we are not disqualified (2 Cor. 13:5-6).

It is one thing to be made alive to the reality of Christ everywhere, but what about realizing His presence is within? This dramatically changes our reality. You were never disqualified.

He has made a home in you! You can converse with and enjoy Father God in your home and wherever your day finds you. He would love for us to realize this truth all the time; this knowledge makes life so much more enjoyable.

We may try and convince ourselves that it is our responsibility to cultivate an environment that welcomes God's presence, but He has already cultivated every environment for us through the

---

[3] Lawrence, *The Practice of the Presence of God*, fourth conversation.

Chapter 3

gift of His Son. Pause, look up, listen and feel the reality of our omnipresent God who has sent His Holy Spirit into every nook and cranny of our human experience, even this experience we call motherhood.

Thankfully the Lord is not going to avoid gracing you with His presence just because an intense bout of sibling rivalry broke out and resulted in an injury inflicted by a bigger brother. It did interrupt your *quiet time,* but He didn't disengage from your life. When a call from the nursery interrupts your deep spiritual moment in a church service because your baby had a huge diaper blow out, *don't worry*, you didn't miss out on God when you went to change your baby. His presence followed you all the way out of the sanctuary and into the loud nursery. In fact, He was never absent to begin with.

The truest solitude is not something outside you, not an absence of men or of sound around you: it is an abyss opening up in the center of your own soul.
– Thomas Merton.[4]

---

[4] Thomas Merton, *Seeds of Contemplation* (New Directions, 1987 ed.), 59.

36

Chapter 4
The Practice of Daily Wonder
... and enjoying God in the natural

God writes the Gospel not in the Bible alone, but also on trees, and in the flowers and clouds and stars.
– Martin Luther

When my first child approached school age, my husband and I decided to home school. We made this decision for no other reason than we thought it would be a good fit for our family. We traveled a lot and liked the idea and freedom of taking school with us wherever we needed to go. At the time, homeschooling was totally foreign to me. I was eager for as much advice as possible on teaching my kids at home. One of the greatest and simplest pieces of advice I was given was this: *Teach your children the love of learning, once they love to learn they are set for life.* I have found this to be very true. A love of learning can open doors for all kinds of untold prospects. A love of learning, coupled with the freedom of time to explore, equals limitless possibilities!

One of my sons is *Mr. Fact Man*. He loves to read about facts and has an apt ability to memorize the most interesting details about the most obscure things. If you were to spend at least 30 minutes with my son, I can almost guarantee you would be informed about something you knew nothing about before the two of you met. You could learn things like: *The Blue-Ringed Octopus is known as the most poisonous octopus, has a venom that can kill an adult human in minutes, and there is no known antidote! Starfish don't have brains. Everyone's tongue print is different. Shrimp's hearts are in their heads. And, the Pyramid of Giza is the result of the accumulation of 2.5 million bricks!*

There is something new to be learned everyday for my little sponges. Sometimes it can be awkward when my children are studying animal facts and they come across details about how the animal species mate. All parents have been there, *right?* Recently we were informed about the black widow that devours the male spider after they mate. My son told us about this mating ritual at dinner with friends we didn't know so well. It was awkward.

I love watching my children learn about this world. I feel so privileged to learn alongside of them. I feel so much more enlightened because of their hunger for knowledge and their eagerness to share their new findings with me.

As we learn about our surroundings, as we open books and study facts and discoveries, everything seems to point to God. Everything! Every little detail, design and natural instinct is all so perfectly planned and purposeful. Nature is miraculous! The familiarity of it all shouldn't negate the magic of it all. I am talking about everyday, run-of-the-mill life events here, even the stuff we get so bored with. If we choose to be present and pay attention we can learn a lot about eternity and our Creator. There is a story God is telling you in the butterfly, in the rivers and even in the macaroni and cheese you had for dinner. We can be aware, and we can encourage our children to listen. Children seem to be naturally *tuned in* anyway. It would be good if we could follow their lead.

Child-like: **marked by innocence, trust and ingenuousness**
Won-der: **a cause of astonishment or admiration**
(Merriam-Webster Dictionary)

Child-like wonder is something I would never like to live without. I love seeing my children get excited about something new, something they have never seen. Remember their first trip to the sea or their first Christmas? There is nothing like the excitement in a three-year-old boy when he catches his first fish. How fun to have children who are not spoiled by experience. Children are so alive! They remind us how exciting and mystical this planet is.

Chapter 4

We grow. We get busy. New things and new discoveries become old news. Everything around us is amazing and so many of us just don't care.

Sometimes I find myself not caring. I get comfortably numb and focused on a routine or schedule, and I forget to live. I don't want to not care. I don't want to get bored. I want to stay appreciative and in awe of everything around us.

I want to give my kids permission to stop everything to study the spider web on the front porch, decorated with tiny jewels from the morning rain. To stop and appreciate the spider's busy work when I am rushing out for an errand seems so impractical in the moment, but when we take a few seconds to appreciate the little things, it makes life better. Living connected is a conscious choice.

Just the other day my son caught a fly, ripped off its head and put it under a microscope to study its eyeball. I was disgusted and very busy making dinner. But when he made me stop what I was doing for a moment to come take a look, I was fascinated at all the dimensions and parts of the fly's eye! I am glad he was so persistent in making me pause from my cooking because now I have a new appreciation for insect eyes!

While there is a time to put away microscopes and fly heads to wash your hands for dinner, I hope most of my children's childhood is spent with ample freedom and time to fill their healthy curiosity. I want to raise responsible, hardworking, organized and successful participants of society, but never at the expense of becoming numb and uninterested in this world and what lies beyond.

I love to think of nature as an unlimited broadcasting station through which God speaks to us every hour, if we will only tune in. – George Washington Carver

Chapter 4

The exciting thing for us as parents is that we not only get to encourage our kids and allow them time to marvel, wonder and be inquisitive about this awesome world around us. We also get to point them to a real God and Creator who designed it all.

I love visiting state parks or viewing a beautiful place with my kids in public and openly discussing how awesome God is for creating such a place. Gazing up at a redwood tree in a crowded California state park and hearing my little girl say, "Wow! God is so cool to have made such huge trees!" For as long as I am living, as long as I am a parent and when I become a grandma, I am going to take children out in nature to study tiny bugs and gaze up at huge Sequoias and storm clouds. And I am going to tell them Who imagined it all.

I love nature! There is something about nature that revives and rejuvenates me. I love being outside, especially with my children. I love putting away our computers and devices, leaving the house and all the chores behind for the day, to go and explore. I love being immersed and mesmerized by something natural, even though we may have seen a million similar trees or flowers or sunsets, there are those amazing moments when you know God is speaking to you through His creation. I can't tell you how many times I have been out walking with the kids and something natural will happen – something will catch my eye, and in that one little thing, in that one little random moment, the Lord will speak to me so clearly. This is what our walk with Christ is supposed to be about.

The miracle of relationships

Relationships and family are the most miraculous things I can think of. To see a family and community functioning in love for one another has had more impact on my faith than anything I have ever experienced. The love between my husband and I is a miracle. My children and the love we have for each other is a miracle. The reconciliation between a severed and torn family is a miracle. I have witnessed so much deep transformation in people when they encounter God's love. There is nothing like

40

seeing someone shed years of resentment and bitterness. It is miraculous.

One of the primary inspirations for writing this book was the desire to awaken something inside us that values the relationships within a family. The people that make up your family and communities are so important.

Somewhere along the line of church history we forgot the constant reality of God at work among and within us. It seems in most minds that God is far from our daily existence and we are just biding our time here on earth till we can go, "to a better place." We've started schools, organized conferences and written enough books to bore the most boring book worm all about striving to reach the supernatural. Which of course is great – people need to know the endless possibilities of God Almighty, but what I want to know is do we also apply as much attention to the more frequent miracles that happen every day among us? Do we discard them as "common" or "natural" things – things that are meant to be a constant source of wonder and amazement to men?" – Benjamin Dunn[5]

We sometimes have a fear if we acknowledge that everything, even the ordinary love between two people, is a miracle, than nothing will truly seem miraculous.

While I remain expectant and desire to see the Lord move in a supernatural, out-of-the-ordinary way, in healings, visions and unexplainable miracles, I am most satisfied and filled with awe when people love one another. Love is the greatest manifestation; everything else is secondary.

Remaining content in the little things is key. Receiving the greatest gift of all – Christ's life, death and resurrection – will

---

[5] Benjamin Dunn, *Lamb, Wine and a Divine Comedy* (Santa Cruz, CA: Joy Revolution, 2012), 57.

awaken you with the supernatural within the natural life, highlighting what is valuable and truly important: the people in your life.

There is a reason you are here on this planet, living this life in your *meat sacks.* Don't wish time away. You have been created for a supernatural purpose. The Bible says, *even the angels envy us* (Heb. 1, 1 Peter 1:12). Getting to encounter the Gospel in our natural state is envied! Don't miss out on *now!* Don't forsake this human experience. What you are participating in right now is so important.

Once we cannot recognize Christ in natural everyday life within a community then we have missed the importance of our time here. We are eternal and this life is *but a vapor,* but that vapor is part of our eternity, a very wonderful, integral part.

Jesus with His skin on
My daughter, when she was about four years old, was praying and out of frustration said, "I want to see Jesus mom!"

"You can see Jesus, just close your eyes," I said.

"No, I want to see Him with His skin on!"

We were meant to experience *Jesus with His skin on.* To crave something real and tangible, to connect with our faith, is a healthy desire. I don't want a figurative, elusive Jesus in the sky. I want what my daughter was bold enough to ask for: *Jesus with His skin on.* I want to touch, taste, smell and see Him every day! I want to see Him in my husband, in my children, in the community I live in. I want to see him in the messy, dirty matter that we come in contact with every day. His Spirit was sent to fill the earth, and He came to live within. We have become *"Jesus with His skin on."*

   ... as He is, so also are we in this world (1 John 4:17).

Chapter 4

I am so thankful Jesus came to us, fully God and fully man. For good reason He didn't leave out that *flesh* part when he humbly came as a man for all men in the incarnation. He gazed at the same stars. He felt thirst and hunger and fatigue. He experienced the monotony of a chore. He put his hands in the dirt and saw the seasons change. He experienced a mother's love and a friend's rejection. To think of our Lord with His skin on, coming in flesh and dying in flesh, awakens me to the Glory meant to be found in our world and our everyday lives.

As you go, preach this message: "The Kingdom of Heaven is near" (Matthew 10:7).

When I encounter God and His glory in the natural, I get to catch a glimpse of Heaven. Heaven is near. When I am looking to see God in everything, I find the balance I crave. It's not a balance that craves a little spirituality and a little something natural, but a balance that finds that the two are intertwined. In the same way that Christ was fully man and fully God, our life is meant to be fully natural and fully supernatural all at the same time. We do not seek out Heaven apart from earth at the same time; we watch the two collide. How beautiful to see the spirituality in the simple and ordinary. When we realize that what we are doing now is part of the whole of eternity, then time takes on a completely different meaning.

Chapter 5
The Practice of Gratitude
… and cultivating a thankful heart

*I would maintain that thanks are the highest form of thought,
and that gratitude is happiness doubled by wonder.*
– G.K Chesterton

I don't rely on one specific list of tricks and guidelines in dealing with parenting issues, and my purpose for writing this book was never to introduce a bunch of parenting *techniques* to new mothers. But I do have one simple practice that seems to work in matters of sibling rivalry, or even when a kid just seems to be in a crummy mood.

Hypothetical situation: Let's just say my little angels are fighting in the back seat of the car, and before I can count to 10 a simple argument has escalated into hitting and name-calling – a lot of hitting and name-calling! My initial instinct is to chime in with, "Hey! You guys better stop or I'll …" (fill in the blank with some sort of terrible consequence). My children will stop the backseat battle because they have been reprimanded and threatened with a punishment, but inside they are still angry with each other, and probably also angry with me.

But seeing through a lens of grace and gratitude is the true key to diffusing these legal squabbles. I stop the argument, and then I often do something like this: I will have each of the parties involved list 10 positive traits that they are thankful for in their sibling. At first they are hesitant. Number one on the list may be something ridiculous like, "I am thankful that we don't share a room!"

"No," I say, "what is something you are thankful for about who they are? What do you like about their personality that makes them a wonderful sister or brother to have?"

Chapter 5

"Well, I like that they can be funny."

"Good," I say. "What else?"

"I like their laugh and the way they smile. I like when we play in the water together and pretend we are on a deserted island alone."

Before you know it the list changes from a hesitant kid being forced to mumble compliments to his sister, to a kid that is inspired with love and appreciation for her. The whole mood and relational vibe in the car becomes completely transformed. We all realize, *wow, we really like each other!*

I do the same thing with a grumpy and complaining little stinker. I say, "What are ten things you are thankful for?" (And I am not expecting some deep, grandiose statement of appreciation from my six-year-old like, *I am thankful for the reconciliation of the world through the death of our Savior!*) I just let them find their own words of appreciation. Anything, even simple things suffice.

"I am thankful for my Lego guy."

"Good, what else?"

"I am thankful for pizza, for you and Dad and for my friends."

"Those are great things in your life; you really have a lot to be grateful for, don't you?"

Before that list of 10 is complete, my little grump is radiating with gratitude. Nothing satisfies and fills my mommy heart – and fills a home with joy and peace – like children who are thankful and content. I have to remember this practice for myself. The next time I am feeling sorry for myself and unthankful, I can stop to consider the things that I am thankful for. That should straighten me up in no time!

46

Chapter 5

It is good to give thanks to the Lord, to sing praises to your name, O Most High; to declare your steadfast love in the morning, and your faithfulness by night (Psalm 92:1-2 ESV).

Thankfulness is a key ingredient and the icing on the cake. For all things sweet in this life, you will find gratitude at the base, source, core and root.

I can be so busy and focused on things that have to get done that I forget to appreciate life. Then suddenly something will catch my eye, even if I have seen it a million times before. Out of the blue, I find myself overwhelmed by appreciation for a sunset or a hug from one of my children. When we express gratitude throughout our day, we can find ourselves entranced by a substance that seems to stop time and halt us in our busy tracks, like someone slipped a little something into our drink. Suddenly we'll find we can't stop expressing thanks. Everything radiates goodness under the drink of gratitude, drawing out of us endless praise. This is when life is really good.

While it is tempting to wake up in the morning, heavy with a list of to-do's, grumbling at the idea of doing chores and dealing with whining kids, if we make it a priority to declare our thankfulness, the whole heart of our day will take on a tone that refuses to look at or take notice of any negativity. Thankfulness gives us a rhythm and pace that makes our days and lives seem supernaturally easy – even our harder days. Declaring *His steadfast love in the morning and His faithfulness by night* will change any negative perception of reality. Reality is, He is always good.

Gratitude looks good on you!
I firmly believe that it is absolutely impossible to remain unhappy when one is thankful. Just try it; right now think of at least 10 things you are thankful for, even little things like coffee in the morning (that is usually on the top of my list). I bet the whole countenance of your face will change as the list evolves in your head and your heart follows along. Try to think of 10

Chapter 5

more things, and then 20 more. What you were stressed about earlier will seem silly next to the list of goodness in your life. If even a twinge of unhappiness remains, I would be surprised. Practicing gratitude has to be the best way to overcome despondency, depression, heavy heartedness, anger, pride, jealousy or insecurity. You name it; gratitude is the antidote to your problems.

A simple exercise of meditating on the simple things you are thankful for can, when regularly practiced, grow into a constant state of simply *being happy and content*. Gratitude will become a habit, which will produce a deep substance of joy. As the French educator, Jean Baptiste Massieu wrote, "Gratitude is the memory of the heart." A habit of joy is formed, when fed by a habit of thankfulness.

I am confident of this, when thankfulness fills the heart it will really change your entire life. It will transform your whole perspective on everything.

Thankfulness has a source

> Therefore, just as you received the Messiah Yeshua as Lord, keep living your life united with him. Remain deeply rooted in him; continue being built up in him and confirmed in your trust, the way you were taught, so that you overflow in thanksgiving (Col. 2:6-7, CJB).

I don't say, "thank you" when I am wronged. I am not full of gratitude when the meter-man hands me a parking ticket. Thanksgiving really only comes as the result of having received something we know is a good gift, right?

As a believer we have been given the greatest gift of all! This gift is supposed to be realized as the source and foundation of our whole human experience. This gift we received, in Christ, is what solidifies and connects us to the things in which we take pleasure and find joy.

48

Chapter 5

There is no greater gift than one man's life. The gift of Christ's death funded every aspect of our lives; every trial and every joyful experience has been paid for. Even if you are unable to see something beautiful in a difficult time, a simple *thanks* may be the secret solution to your obstacle. Dig through the rubble and mess with a thankful heart and find the joy that makes life sweet and worth living again. Don't give up! Be persistent in finding the gift of Christ in everything you encounter.

Has life been weighing us mothers down? Are you noticing a dull, colorless, flat mood to your days? As mothers we crave to feel alive; our children crave that kind of "awake" presence in their home. Thankfulness allows us to welcome life into our home. Thankfulness enables us to see Grace blanketing our family. When you make a choice each day to be in a state of thankfulness, your home will radiate vital life.

There is always a reason to practice gratitude. In the middle of everything that comes your way, see your gift of salvation. Regardless of my circumstances, because I know who I am in Christ, I can *overflow with thanksgiving.* When we are overflowing with thanksgiving, we are overflowing with joy; and when we have arrived at joy, we have found true rest.

Expressing thanks is not even optional as a believer; it is imperative to live the victorious Christian life.

Thankfulness is not *putting on your happy face so no one knows you're miserable.* Thankfulness is a choice to recognize a good gift. When we received Christ it was with two words, *thank you!* It should be with those same two words that we choose to live our lives. Teach your children those two words and, most importantly, remind them what we are eternally thankful for. If I have taught my children to find thanks in everything, if I have helped them form a habit of thankfulness, if gratitude is always at the tip of their tongue, then I have done my job as a parent.

Chapter 5

Thank-you as a prayer

Do not be anxious about anything, but in every situation, by prayer and petition, with thanksgiving, present your requests to God. And the peace of God, which transcends all understanding, will guard your hearts and your minds in Christ Jesus (Phil. 4:6-7 NIV).

Thanksgiving is not a mere legalistic, external exercise. It is a *change of thinking* – a practice of internally recognizing reality from God's perspective. When we pray as a family, it feels good to know that we are not groveling and begging for something we need. All we have and could possibly need is found completed in Christ. Prayer becomes a thank you, even in the middle of asking.

If the only prayer you ever say in your whole life is "thank you," that would suffice
– Meister Eckhart

Thank you is a complete prayer, whether it's a simple conversation with the Lord, or a desperate cry from your heart for your family.

I love the habit of living in conversational prayer. Prayer is powerful! It works! But what has evoked a hope and trust that this God will even hear us? Why do we even converse? I suspect it is because we believe He is really good. He is good and cares because He died that all would be whole and well. He died that you would be whole and well! We pray the prayer of thanks, to remember what we already have in Him. To know what He has done is to know you lack nothing, even in your toughest hour.

Thank you Lord for what You have already done and how it changes everything that we know.

Thank You for Your grace in this life and in every situation.

50

Chapter 5

Thank You for Your perspective.

Thank You for fulfilling all Your promises in my life, my husband's life and in the life of my children.

Thank You that You care about every detail, and that You know all my longings and dreams before they are even realized.

Thank You for showing me Your purposes, even when I feel purposeless.
You are good Lord, always.

Thank You!

Chapter 6
The Practice of Optimism
... and overflowing with hope

The *Webster's Dictionary* defines optimism as: *an inclination to put the most favorable construction upon actions and events or to anticipate the best possible outcome.*

"Glass half full, or half empty?" This is what many of us think of when we hear the word, *optimism.* Many believers have an understanding of what it means to be optimistic. I believe that having an optimistic outlook on life is not an option as a believer in the Gospel. If the Lord is always good, always victorious and always in a good mood, like scripture states He is, then we have to view our circumstances with the hope that, because our life is found in Him, all of our situations will always end positively. His glass is always full and overflowing.

I have always been optimistic by nature. I remember, even as a young girl, refusing to acknowledge negative things going on around me. I did this not so much from a state of denial, but more as a way to find protection in an unstable home. I really believe my ability to avoid focusing on negativity was birthed out of my faith in Jesus at a young age.

Once, when I was five, I remember a friend of mine drowned in a lake near our home in Coeur d'Alene, Idaho during a church picnic. I remember being totally un-phased and at peace when her dad scooped her lifeless, pale body onto the shore and began CPR. Everyone around me seemed to be in a state of panic, but I knew she would be all right. She soon started to cough up water, regain consciousness and lived to tell the story.

In some ways optimism became a defense mechanism for me as a little girl. I would insist that my parents had a great marriage, even knowing full well that my father was having a relationship with another woman. I would also use my positive outlook to isolate myself from conflict. I had more of an *"ignorance is bliss"* approach to things. If someone said something mean to me, I would pretend not to hear or be affected. I think I still do this; it works for me. Being optimistic saved me from focusing on negative things while growing up in a broken family. Optimism also kept me from harboring a lot of bitterness. While a mental behaviorist may disregard this as avoiding reality, it is really just a matter of selectively *choosing* positive things to focus upon.

> *Finally, brothers and sisters, whatever is true, whatever is noble, whatever is right, whatever is pure, whatever is lovely, whatever is admirable – if anything is excellent or praiseworthy – think about such things* (Phil. 4:8, NIV).

Sometimes my optimism would anger my more *realistic* siblings and friends. Even to this day, I frustrate some with my positive approach to life because I refuse to validate their negativity. Some may feel I need to be more objective and "honest" about situations. Maybe if I were studying life as a clinical, Freudian psychologist, I guess I would need to be more objective. But when I am studying the Gospel, hope seems to override what may seem realistic at the time.

I know someone who gets so annoyed with me for refusing to regularly watch the news, but I don't look forward to watching the news. If more good stories were broadcast that would be one thing, but the majority of the stories are negative. And negative news often manipulates society to behave accordingly. To tune in to that much negativity on a daily basis is not healthy. Years ago, people would focus much more on their local community, what was going on with their neighbors and families. I believe it is important to be aware of what is going on in our world, but I also think that for the average young mother, raising little kids and nurturing a home, focusing on the crises around the globe can feel debilitating at times. I have found that, as a mom, it is not being ignorant to keep my eyes on our

Chapter 6

own family and community. Focusing here first is fruitful. Make a difference where you are able. If every person would start with the one in front of him or her, there would actually be real global change. Sometimes it can be easier to focus on the negativity in other places and in others' lives – and perhaps that is the real escapism. It is a way to escape noticing growth needed in ourselves and the change we are capable of bringing within our communities. Be informed, but if you start to feel weighed down by another tragic news story, it may be time to change the station.

Optimism is imperative in the Christian life
Optimism transcends the *glass is half full* attitude. Optimism births a positive reality out of a determined state of mind that focuses on a positive outcome, even if things aren't going well. Without this outlook on life, we miss hope, and without hope, just like scripture says, we perish. In the middle of every war, peril and collapse there has always been the optimist that breathes new life. Without an optimistic speech from leaders or internal voices, we would give up and surrender to the negative.

Optimism is far more than a character or personality trait. I steadfastly believe that there need be no separation between the realist and the optimist. *I am realistically optimistic.* In other words, I am a realist who is also an optimist, in that I choose to look at the situation honestly and purpose to direct it towards the best possible outcome. However, I do believe there is a very distinct separation between the mind of the optimist and the mind of the pessimist. But the mindset is not, and should not be attributed to, a personality type, especially for the believer. Optimism is imperative for the Christian life. I am not only positive because of my personality type; I am an positive because of my hope in Christ. While every camp of thought and theory may have their *dreamers* and their *realists,* both camps can err on the side of hope even while one may seem more extravagant than the other. I would much rather shoot for extravagant hope, rather than play it safe and settle for the worst-case scenario.

Chapter 6

Being optimistic is brave. When we are optimistic, we can boldly remain joyful and empower those around us to think of the best possible outcome in the most difficult times.

An optimistic Gospel

Scriptures are full of optimism. You won't find a pessimist preaching the Gospel in the New Testament. Something about, *It is finished! Death is conquered!* rings with a happy tone.

In our homes and as we raise our children the Gospel applies to every bad day and situation. We can remind our kids that the Gospel applies to everything, and our reaction and response to trials can resonate with His victory. Make a hopeful response a habit. Pass on this habit of optimism. I admit that having to look at a seemingly insurmountable mountain of laundry each day doesn't always translate into positive thoughts. But we will always have something in our life that may seem insurmountable at the time. For now, I am glad that it is mostly just laundry, dishes and home school for me. I don't have to remind anyone that there are some families around us facing terminal illnesses or job lay-offs.

Even with all that seems daunting in life, a positive outlook is a legacy of the Gospel in our homes. This doesn't mean I overlook a hard situation as if it is nothing to sweat about. When those around us are struggling, we are called to walk in compassion and understanding for one another, not out of a place of duty, but out of a place of God-given love. *Be compassionate just as your Father is compassionate.* If my child or a friend is hurt, I am compelled, out of love, to comfort them. We are called to *rejoice with those who rejoice and weep with those who weep.* But even as we meet those in tragedy, our objective is always to lift their vision back to a place of hope.

Recently, a dear friend of mine went through a cycle where every turn of events seemed worse than the first. It was very hard to watch my normally optimistic friend cope with such a hard time. During each conversation I had with her, I would try to say every positive thing that I could think of to encourage her. I began to get tired of hearing myself say, "It is going to get better, everything will work out," when things just seemed to get worse and worse. There had been about a year's worth of *unlucky* events and she was out of steam, broken and very vulnerable. One day she lost it while talking with me. "I just need you to listen to me and validate what is going on in my life right now. I don't need you to make it better," she said. She was right; I didn't need to try and make her situation seem like it wasn't happening or even try and pretend like it wasn't really terrible. Sometimes when we are helping someone go through a hard time, we can feel an urgency to make it all better. When I am consoling my husband or teenager after a hard, disappointing day, my first instinct is to try and make everything better as quickly as possible. We never like to see the ones we love hurt. While we may be really anxious to see our friends and loved ones in a place where things are running smoothly for them, we have to remember that our biggest encouragement for them comes from a place of hope amid the crisis, even if that crisis seems to drag on. The power of hope and optimism is unafraid to recognize something really terrible for what it is. You can say, "That sucks! It's so hard and terrible and ugly and wrong!" Acknowledging a trial and validating someone who is going through a hard time doesn't mean you are participating or encouraging a pity party. Your understanding just gains the trust of a friend, a spouse, or a child who is vulnerable. It opens a way for you to speak truth and hope over their life. Hope just highlights the bigger picture. Hope gives us a glimpse of eternity. You may not always have the answers and steps to security, but your hope is enough. Hope is always accessible through our victory in Christ's death and resurrection. We have a victorious and hopeful destination. That is reality.

Misery loves company

They say *misery loves company*. This is quite true. I have met people who seem very determined to stay unhappy – and they are persistent in their goal to convince you everything around us is just plain miserable. Even Eeyore, in *Winnie the Pooh,* would rather have a friend to share in his grumbling than a friend to share in joy.

Joy loves company too! You don't hear that cliché often. Joy loves to celebrate with others. When we have good news, we instinctively want to share it with someone; it is so wonderful to have a friend to share in your joy.

The last thing the world needs is another reason to stay depressed, pop another pill or check out from what connects them to the substance of joy in life. A negative outlook usually leads to despair; despair leads to depression and a disconnection from the joys in life and in our relationships. I would like to be joyfully connected. I would like my children and family and friends to share in the same joy. I hope to always be the kind of mother and friend that is able to navigate through temporal circumstances by staying focused on the eternal joy set before us. You are a voice of optimism and hope as a believer in your homes and among the people that surround you. With this in mind, you should surround yourself with optimistic and hopeful people who are eager to share in your joy and to have you share in theirs. At times, I have had to separate and distance myself from people that fed into negativity around me, especially people who put a negative spin on circumstances in my life or my family's life. The people that are inclined to point out the joy set before you are the people you want surrounding you and your family. These people will make up a community that strengthens your family.

Christ's hope forges a path for the greatest life imaginable. The glass is always *overflowing!*

The Practice of Building in Wisdom
... and being architects of our own homes

The wise woman builds her house, but with her own hands the foolish one tears it down (Prov. 14:1, NIV)

I recently went to a science museum with the kids where we toured many scientific exhibits. One section of the exhibit was based on *social contagion*, a term for moods spreading from person to person. The example given in one particular exhibit was on the theory of yawns being contagious. As an experiment, they had individuals sit in a booth and watch a series of clips of different people yawning to see if it also triggered a yawn in the viewers. In a similar booth there were clips of people laughing. I sat in each booth and found myself both yawning and laughing! The point of this ongoing experiment was to demonstrate how our moods might be affected, as a society, by the environment and people around us, especially how our moods might trigger certain behaviors or mannerisms like a yawn or a smile.

I couldn't forget the whole concept of this simple science exhibit at the museum as I drove home that day. I began to really think about the truth of *social contagion,* especially how it relates to our personal lives and local community. This is more than a psychosomatic "mind over matter" theory – humans really have a spiritual influence upon one another. It seems so true and applicable to me as a mother and leader in my home and also as part of a community. In an empowering sense, we have the ability to change and affect the environment we live in for the good, whether it is our work scene, our school campus, the public atmosphere around us, or a woman's most sacred arena, her home.

Have you ever heard the saying, *If you see someone without a smile, give them yours*? Our joy, peace and love are contagious!

Chapter 7

I would like to take the theory of *social contagion* and apply it to my home, hoping to spread a smile rather than a frown. We have been given such divine roles as mothers and wives in our homes. We are not just participating in setting the mood of the home, but we are also structurally building a family on a daily basis. In a sense, we are *family architects*.

Whether you are aware of this or not, we set a tone and flavor for our whole household. The mood of the house tends to follow mom's lead. As goes the mom, so goes the house. Our children and our husband can be like an orchestra we are conducting. Go ahead and call yourself *maestro,* if you like.

We can bring a nurturing flavor of joy, peace, order, inspiration, comfort, warmth and encouragement to our home and make it feel like a private Hawaiian oasis in the middle of a frozen Alaskan winter. On the flip side, we also have the ability to create a negative home environment. There is nothing worse than one of my irritable days, when I am acting like something that rhymes with *itch*. The whole household can suffer at the expense of mom's bad mood. I have found myself both building my home up and, on occasion, knocking it down like a demolition truck.

What is our goal?
What are we building each day as we direct and nurture our homes? I need a goal for my family. When I am winging it all the time, I can feel directionless. I want to have a plan and a target. Having a rhythm for my home, in each season, seems to pace my family so we don't burn out. I want to understand why the little things I do each day for my family are a priority over a full-time career or ventures outside the home. I know that it is not all pointless, but I still want to be reminded, *why?* Knowing the value of what I am working towards and laboring to build will give me a reason to persevere in what seems to be never-ending. I have been at this mothering thing for 16 years now, and the role and greatness of demand for what I do on a daily basis for my family seems to only increase as my children get

older. Without a goal, vision and inspiration from a greater source, I may be tempted to *throw in the towel* at times!

Recently, I sat and had coffee with a friend. She is an older mom and a grandma now. Her family and all their accomplishments are the envy of many in our community.

I look at all the framed photos on her mantle: the births, the graduations and the weddings. It all looks so easy in a picture frame. I want to know what she did to raise such wonderful children. Can she recommend some good books? Is there a concrete piece of advice she can send me home with that I can apply to my own family? She mentions some good books out there that helped her a little, but nothing extraordinarily life changing. She also opens up and shares about some hard things her children had to go through. "Life is unpredictable," she says. "You have to find what works best for your always changing family."

I honestly love this woman. I love her humility and how she is able to admit family life isn't something you can always narrow down and perfect in one parenting book or even one lifetime. She didn't brag that she has it all figured out. She just encouraged me to keep a good sense of humor and trust the Lord for direction. I left her house feeling empowered by her honesty and by the example of someone who has learned to trust. Her vulnerability in sharing the fact that there is no perfect answer inspires me to trust God for all those details I simply have not yet figured out.

Even though I know it is helpful to adapt a routine or template of disciplines that make up a functional family, the unpredictability of my home reminds me that awareness and sensitivity to Holy Spirit's daily direction will always be my greatest navigation system. There is a gift in the always changing and unpredictable family life. The gift is that we will be constantly provoked to search for guidance from our Heavenly Father. I hope to always remain so sensitive and trusting that directions given in whispers can be heard over the loudest chaos. There has been no event or circumstance that has made me appreciate and grow more keenly dependent on Holy Spirit's voice than being a mom to such precious children.

I want to always remember that building a home is fluid, always moving and filling up new spaces and shapes. A family is always in perpetual motion, so I need to be prepared to change, mold and expand my perspective. I would like what I am building to stand as a solid constitution for centuries to come. I would like for the uniqueness and quality and craftsmanship to last and be admired for generations. I don't want to just "wing-it" with my family. I need a plan! A goal! I need wisdom.

I know nothing pleases God more than faith. To ask Him for wisdom is a righteous request, so it is only fitting that a mom, walking in faith, be bold enough to ask for wisdom whenever she needs it, "But let him ask in faith, with no doubting, for the one who doubts is like a wave of the sea that is driven and tossed by the wind" (James 1:6, NLT).

I can totally picture myself, *like a wave of the sea that is driven and tossed by the wind,* when I don't walk in wisdom, simply because I am hesitant to ask. I am confident that wisdom, when yeilded to in complete trust, will provide us the tools and perfect design for our families. Wisdom may sound and look a lot different than we expect, simplifying something we may overcomplicate without even realizing it.

As my first-born grew and her many talents started emerging, I quickly realized that God had blessed me with quite a genius of a child. She was good at just about everything she did. She excelled academically, artistically and athletically. I remember being a bit burdened and intimidated as the mother of this amazing kid. I wondered how I should foster the growth and development of all her unique gifts. *What lessons should I put her in? Should I send her to some advanced learning school? Should I focus on one skill or be as diverse as possible?* At the time, she was only seven, but I didn't want to blow it. Here I was feeling completely unequipped to facilitate stimulation for this brilliant child. I sat there contemplating what I should do with her and asking God for wisdom when I clearly felt Holy Spirit nudge me and say, "*Just focus on having her make her bed every day for now.*" Here I was thinking I needed to quickly sign her up for violin and Mandarin, and Holy Spirit told me to have her make her bed! I realized that He wanted me to teach her the little things in life that build character. He showed me that my daughter needed the discipline of everyday chores and practices that would grow and build the character that she would need to one day do great things. Now that my daughter is a big teenage girl, I see all the fruit and the humility that came from the daily disciplines of little things like bed making. I see character in her that will take all the talents God has put inside her to their full potential.

I am so thankful for direction and the ability all of us moms have been given to hear clearly for our children. We are able to hear *bed making* when others are saying *violin lessons*. Asking for an answer is not always the same as asking for wisdom. Wisdom is more than an answer; Wisdom is the Spirit that will direct us in the fulfillment of promises within each one of us. There is something so specific in God's wisdom that will sound so different from the wisdom of men. If you need wisdom, *ask!*

Wisdom has built her house
Proverbs 9:1 tells us that "Wisdom has built her house." Consider that this is *past tense*. The wisdom necessary for the construction and completion of your unique home *has* already been made available. *By wisdom the Lord laid the earth's foundations* (Prov. 3:19ₐ NIV).

It is ultimately the Lord establishing our homes through us by means of His wisdom. Wisdom is the perfect gift of grace, and this grace has been made accessible to every mother on a daily basis through the person of Jesus Christ. Although we may face a lot of unpredictability in building our home (I am almost certain we all do) wisdom is always at hand for us. Recognize this wisdom rooted in His grace when you structure your day, and you will be surprised at just how skilled and equipped you will become. We have to trust His grace working through us and remember who is really building our home. When we know His wisdom and grace, it will be harder to find ourselves in that frazzled, frustrated state that usually leads to demolition!

There is a unique design and artistry that make up our families that separate us from others' homes. There is a flavor and a completely different feel when I walk into another family's home. I even love how each home has a specific smell. Wisdom will begin to be personified, as our home is customized and handcrafted by Holy Spirit through each of us! We can learn from other families. I love the wisdom I gain from other women, but God has something specific for your home and He wants to show you.

Freedom from burdensome ideals
A while back I was sitting at a birthday party for one of my children's friends just listening to the moms talk:

One mom is going back and forth from Italian to English as she converses with her five-year-old. She is Chinese, so in all her children probably speak three languages. Another mom is telling the story of how she made the gluten-free, no-refined-sugar cupcakes for the party, "I had to be very patient while making these cupcakes! I accidently broke my last two eggs so I had to sit and wait for my chickens to lay more eggs!" She went on explaining the complexity of her cupcakes, "The frosting has no food coloring in it, I used the juice from a beet in my garden to give it that red color."

I was speechless. That takes baking to a whole different level for me. I was even a little envious at the care this mom took to be all healthy and natural for the birthday party. I thought to myself, *maybe I should get chickens and use beet juice to dye my treats from now on.* Then I looked over at the cupcakes, all sad looking, dense and not so much red but a brownish burgundy color, and I thought, *Nah!*

We can busy ourselves with so much unimportant stuff. You moms probably know what I mean. Maybe you read the latest *Martha Stewart* magazine and feel the need to reorganize every shelf in your house with alphabetical labels, or sew special pillowcases with intricate embroidered initials for each of your children. Maybe you heard the other mothers talking about soccer practice, lacrosse team, basket weaving classes and calligraphy lessons, followed up by Cantonese language lessons, and you feel like you need to keep up with them. Or maybe you are making sure every bite of food your family takes is certified organic, dye free, GMO free, cage free and packaged in all recycled containers. Parenting ideals have become so ridiculously extreme. They change from one generation to the next. There are so many blogs, pins, shows and magazines with more great ideas than we know what to do with. Just when I have found the perfect candy to cook for Christmas, a better recipe will be up on the Internet faster than I can say, *jam thumbprints!* And jam thumbprints are hard to beat!

Don't forget all the other really good ways to "serve for Christ" as well. We can volunteer in the nursery and at soup kitchens, put together care kits for the homeless, or make another meal for the mom who just had her fifth baby. I would love to open my home to foster children someday. John and I already have two children's homes in India, and I feel guilty for not visiting the children there more often! The fact is, there are so many *good* things we could be doing for others, but we have to pause and ask God what to focus on for now. We can't do it all, especially all at once. *One thing at a time moms ... one thing at a time.*

Ask God to show you what is *yours* and what is just a good idea. He knows your heart and your good intentions. I am full of good intentions! But I also get burned out because I max myself out on too many commitments. My new best friend lately has been a two-letter word, *"No!"*

Not all of those ideals are wrapped in wisdom; some are distractions and dangling carrots propped up by other motives than Holy Spirit. If you are feeling like your home isn't matching the picture in your head, then ask Holy Spirit to highlight the important stuff and identify the *fluff* or unnecessary fillers in your day. He wants you to find that *zone* and rhythm for your family. Sometimes our main obstacle in building our homes (in a way that works for our families) is the unrealistic goals and expectations we have set in our minds for our family and ourselves.

Appreciating your own style

My mom never fussed over her house being perfectly organized and tidy. I remember a plaque on the wall of our kitchen that read, *My house is clean enough to be healthy and messy enough to be happy.* She really lived by that saying. She never got overwhelmed about having every detail perfect when we had company. She just made sure people felt welcomed and comfortable. People felt so relaxed and at home when they came to visit.

My siblings and I always had freedom to do any craft or project we wanted to, at any time. *Mom, can I use the glitter? Sure honey! Mom, can I paint the walls in my room a new color? Sure!* I literally remember being nine years old and painting my walls a new shade.

I am quite lackadaisical in many ways myself as a mom, but mention the word *glitter* and it sends chills down my spine. And kids painting their own walls? Not in a million years!

While I may be a little more particular about what my house looks like, I can really appreciate the creative freedom my mom let us have. To this day I feel so free to create anything at any time. For an artist like myself, that was a huge gift my mom gave me.

Your mother had her strengths and her weaknesses. You have your strengths and weaknesses. Every mother is different in temperament and parenting style. This is part of your design. This will be part of how your home will be structured. It is no mistake that you are *you,* raising a family. Don't strive to be like someone else.

You have your way of doing things as a mom. You have a style and preference, which I am sure has become refined and relaxed with the experience of having kids, but it is still part of who you are as a mom – perfect for your home. You are who you need to be for your kids and your family. Don't beat yourself up because you don't have a knack for baking or a natural love for pets. The fact is, you are gifted in a specific area and that is wonderful! Focus on your strengths and learn to appreciate how that shapes your home. And don't worry; the good Lord will work out your weaknesses. To quote one of my most favorite verses: "But He said to me, 'My grace is sufficient for you, for My power is made perfect in weakness.' Therefore, I will boast all the more gladly about my weaknesses, so that Christ's power may rest on me" (2 Cor. 12:9, NIV).

Loving the Lord and loving others
The value of relationships is the most important thing we are cultivating as a family. The fruit of our spiritual building is the manifestation of a love-saturated environment, where our relationship with God and each other is the most valuable and sacred object. If I find myself trying to rein in an unruly child or bring some order to a hostile home environment, wondering if I need to lay down more rules to whip some kids into shape, it always goes back to the first great command: *Love the Lord your God with all your heart ... and love your neighbor as yourself* (Luke 10:27). And this only happens when we realize that *He first loved us!* (1 John 4:19).

Chapter 7

The other evening, while I was cleaning up after dinner, I overheard my husband break up a fight that erupted between some of the kids. He began to talk to the kids about how loving others should be a primary goal and desire in our hearts. He gave them a simple analogy:

Imagine you are playing a very important game. Everyone collects as many black or red pieces as possible. Throughout the whole game you are convinced that the black pieces are worth the most points, so you focused on winning as many black pieces as possible. At the end of the game you take your big pile of black pieces to be matched with your opponents. You are very confident as you compare your amount next to the rest of the players because you have so many black pieces – way more than the others. Then the game leader announces that the red pieces are of most value. In fact, the black pieces have little to no value at all. You feel so sad at wasting all that time trying to win the black pieces and not caring about collecting the red ones. This is how our life is. The red pieces are love; they are the times we love others. The black pieces are all the extra things we do and chase after. Throughout our lives and when we die, it is only love that is most important.

I loved watching my children really get the concept of *love* being the most valuable thing in our lives as they listened to dad's story. We must have this clear value in our home: *loving others*. And this only happens as we daily recognize God's never-ending love for us.

When we love the Lord and love others, everything falls into place. Love wins! *Keeping the main thing the main thing* is fundamental in building anything that will last for eternity. Essentially we are building character rooted in love in eternal beings – our children. The best foundation for good character in any person will flow out of God's love for us, then our love for Him, followed by a love for others. It is really that simple.

Chapter 7

Your home will be the first template to model forgiveness, patience, trust, servanthood and unconditional love. Your home is where your children will first learn to know how His grace works in this world. Everyday life done around the most familiar people will be the first place where our hearts are tested, and from there, as a family, we are able to reach the world with that same framework established in the home.

The little things you do each day, the disciplines and values you enforce and use to guide your family, they are not just building a home, but they are building communities and society as a whole. What an awesome reality! Persevere parents! I know it is so easy to give up or settle for less than full potential, but you are not just laboring in vain, you are inspired craftswomen. Keep building, your home is looking beautiful! But know it is ultimately the Lord who works so mightily through us.

We do not labor to earn something from God, or even to impress Him. We labor for the simple sake of the joy and pleasure of God within the tasks at hand. We pursue labor for the inherent fun in the call itself. – John Crowder

Chapter 8
The Practice of Letting Go
… and handing over control

As a new mom I remember having a casual conversation with another mother, a much more seasoned mother of six. I am not sure how the topic came up, but I will never forget what she told me. What she nonchalantly shared with me somehow solidified a truth and a freeing perspective on our children *"belonging to us."*

We were observing her children, running around and being busy with their play. I was nursing my newborn and had a preschooler at the time. She said, "You know, our children do not belong to us; we do not own them. The Bible tells us clearly that our husbands belong to us and that we are one flesh. But there is nothing that says our children belong to us."

She wasn't trying to be serious, or intensely spiritual with me. We were just moms hanging out and chatting. But Holy Spirit used her words to highlight how I viewed the ownership of my children. Something in that conversation converted my mind and heart to view my children as completely their own individual selves – entrusted to me but not really *mine* in the sense of ownership. It was and still is such a liberating point of view that this woman gave me, and it has never left.

We are given these children as gifts. They are purposely and thoughtfully given to us to parent. There is a divine connection and supernatural bond of love. They may have your eyes or their father's smile and bushy eyebrows. They may have your inability to keep a beat and dad's sense of humor and wit. But at the end of the day, your son or daughter is an individual. Somewhere you end and they begin, and the other way around.

There is an honoring of your children in that you respect who they are individually. Not in a way that forfeits stewardship and

Chapter 8

obedience to faithfully raise your child before the Lord – but in a way that recognizes how valid and distinct their life is, separate from your own.

We can only clearly see the destiny and purpose in our children when we realize that they are not ours; they are His.

When that mother of six shared this perspective with me so many years ago it seemed so impossible picturing my little infant and preschooler surviving without me. Every aspect of my children's life at that time was fully dependent on me. But now, especially seeing my oldest as a teenager, I can see their individuality clearly setting in. As my children become less and less reliant on me, I have to remind myself that they are fully His just as they have been all along.

... for you did form my inward parts; you did knit me together in my mother's womb (Ps. 139:13, Amplified Translation).

It is amazing to consider how perfectly knit together we all are. When I first read the scripture poetically describing us "knit together," I loved to picture God getting His knitting needles out and setting to work! Every cell and fiber lovingly hand crafted and *knit* together by *His Truly*.

When I was pregnant with my first son, Jonas, I started to miscarry in the early months. I was put on bed rest and warned to stay in bed or I would most likely lose the baby within a short time.

I would lie there in bed hour after hour in our little Alaskan cabin covered in snow, passing time knitting and reading. After a couple weeks of obeying the doctor's orders and staying in bed, while my young preschooler ran circles around me and our house began to show evidence of weeks of accumulated neglect, I knew I had to get up!

Chapter 8

John and I both decided that if this baby was going to go full term it would be beyond our control. I just proceeded with life as usual and by my next check up all was confirmed to be normal! That baby is now a big 12-year-old, brown-eyed boy. He is wonderful, healthy and full of life!

Acknowledging of the fragility of a forming baby in the womb makes any mother stop and think, *This is way out of my control!* Inside of her there is a life of its own. She is just a host. In those first months of pregnancy there is a God-given sense of awe and responsibility that the mom, embracing what is happening in her body, begins to feel. Destiny is forming involuntarily inside of her. It is an outside-of-yourself, out-of-control, unpredictable feeling. You can objectively view the situation and de-mystify what is taking place, but every woman carrying a baby knows that it is a situation beyond herself. I have felt this with all my children, and it is really humbling.

Salvation for the believer can be humbling in a similar way; we realize our weakness and incapability to ensure our own righteousness. We are out of control and our only option is to receive a free gift, or to deny it really exists and is available outside ourselves. We can do a bunch of good, safe and healthy things, but ultimately our salvation and what it produces in our life is not in our hands.

I will praise thee for I am fearfully and wonderfully made: marvelous are thy works; and that my soul knoweth right well (Ps. 139:14, KJV).

I love thinking of all of us as "fearfully made." There is a real sense of trepidation and reverent awe when we reflect on the intricate, minute detail in which every cell and fiber of our being is constructed and held together by God.

The human body is the most unique and complex organism in the world! I can relate with the psalmist David when he wrote Psalm 139. He praises the Creator for how he has been explicitly fashioned. I praise Him for how wonderfully crafted each of my children are. Obviously their Creator has it all under control; down to the tiniest, microscopic detail. *Marvelous are thy works; and that my soul knoweth right well.* Our soul can rest in His works alone.

When someone compliments me for how incredible my children are, I shock them with a bold *"I KNOW!"* I can respond confidently that my children are wonderful, not because I read the right how-to parenting books or strive to be the obedient *Proverbs 31 mother.* But I can always boldly boast in their Creator's hand in their awesome design. I love to admire how remarkable all children are – how amazing and unique and important they are to this world. I may be an encourager by nature, but I will sincerely and genuinely rave about my children or your children. They are truly amazing!

There are times when I am so overcome by praise and adoration for how my children are made. Just in the simplicity of who they are, not in how they have performed or behaved for the day. The feeling will catch me by surprise at the most random moment. It could be something cute they say that is so individual to their personality and perspective, or it may be the way they smirk a certain way that is uniquely trademarked to them. Even the little looks your children give are so distinctive.

Our children are all His unique expressions, fingerprinted perfection, inspected by His grace and marked with approval. They are uniquely *His*, not mine, and we are at liberty to appreciate them! Go ahead and verbally compliment your children; you will be complimenting God as you do.

A human being is like a work of art, the more it is admired the more beautiful it grows reflecting the gift of love like light back to the giver. – Elizabeth Goudge.

Chapter 8

Boys!

I love the nature of a wild at heart boy. Having boys has given me a whole different perspective of *letting go.*

I know a dear friend with six boys! No girls! They are a tribe of vivacious, hungry, wild, tender, precious boys from the ages of 15 down to three. Can you picture their home? The smells? The sights? The toilet? They are all disciplined, polite and loving, but nonetheless, wild boys.

As a mother of two boys who are kinetic daredevils to the core, I am constantly holding my breath or closing my eyes at their latest stunt. I heard one woman joke by saying, "Raising boys is like riding a roller-coaster upside down, backwards in the dark." If you are a mother of a boy you can probably relate to that analogy in one way or another. Even the most mellow and tame male child is full of wonderful unpredictability.

The number of high surfaces my boys have jumped off, sharp objects they have run with, dirty things they have touched and eaten – I would have to say it is a miracle they are alive at the end of each day! I often laughed when my boys were toddlers, "Every day my main goal is to keep my boys alive." It was kind of true!

By the time my eldest son could crawl he could move faster than a Pink Floyd laser show, this way and that way, faster than lightning. I bet with my entire running after him I was probably thinner those days. In addition to his great speed on all fours was the fact that everything went into his mouth; he was always chewing on something random. I would cringe at the foreign mystery objects I would retrieve from his mouth on a daily basis. One day we discovered that his normal breathing pattern sounded a little funny. Rather than a smooth breather, he sounded like a squeaker toy! When we took him in to have him examined and x-rayed they found a small rock lodged deep in his bronchial tube and dangerously close to blocking his windpipe! He had apparently put the rock in his mouth and inhaled it, causing the mysterious squeak. He had emergency surgery to remove the rock. We now have the small rock in his baby book titled *The Six-Thousand-Dollar Rock.*

Boys have become a humorous reminder that even in our best attempts, their safety and well-being is ultimately out of our control.

He really has it all under control

When my oldest was three, she was napping and talking in her sleep. When she woke up I asked her if she was dreaming, because she kept saying, "Jesus. Jesus." Now my daughter was a very articulate little girl, so she was able to tell me her dream in precise detail:

"I was walking on a road with a lot of traffic. God was on one side of me," she said. "I was holding Jesus' hand. I started to let go and run away, and I almost got hit by a car. But Jesus grabbed me and told me to never let go of His hand."

I was a single mother at that time. I was young, foolish in a lot of ways and without the proper tools or ideal circumstances. Her dream gave me such hope in His control and ability in our lives. To sit and hear how Holy Spirit invaded my toddler's naptime to tell her to "never let go of His hand" gave me so much faith in how the Lord works in our lives. She is a teenager now, and I still give her advice and actively parent her. But I know that God has her hand and will remind her to not let go, despite every circumstance and season of her life. He is in control. He has her hand!

Lift up your eyes on high and see! Who has created these? He Who brings out their host by number and calls them all by name; through the greatness of His might and because He is strong in power, not one is missing or lacks anything (Isa. 40:26, AMP).

Chapter 8

It is common for parents to feel so positive and hopeful for their children to succeed in life, in all aspects, when their kids are young and dependent. You gaze upon that perfect, innocent, soft, malleable little child and think, "They will win the Nobel Peace Prize." Then those little children grow up, become independent and live out their choices individually. If they are bad choices, parents seem to always wonder what they did wrong. *Where did I fail?*

The first reaction when a child who goes *off* can be one of fear or guilt, as we reevaluate the past years of parenting. As parents I believe we will make a lot of mistakes, but you can only do for your children what you know how. We do our best based on the revelation that we have been given. But there is grace! You are learning and growing in wisdom alongside your kids, and God has unlimited grace for you to sensitively and faithfully raise and invest in your child. We can believe and expect good fruit for our children. I will always expect the best for my kids, but nothing is 100 percent *fool-proof* in the outcome of their hearts. It may be hard to admit but freeing to do so: *if our children succeed it is not our fault, and if they fail it is not our fault either.*

Be steadfast in your expectations and in directing your children to the love of the Father and a Christ-like life, but remember who is responsible for hearts. If you are a family or part of a community which has witnessed a child "fall away," respond with the same faith and trust that was present when you knew them as little innocent children. If the Lord reveals an area where you blew it with a child, please never be afraid to ask forgiveness. I can't tell you how many times I have had to ask for forgiveness from my kids.

A parent is forever in a state of remembering who is in control. The need for us to acknowledge God's sovereignty and grace over our children (as well as Holy Spirit's ability to lead you as you parent) becomes sustenance in every season of our children's lives within our calling as parents.

Chapter 8

It is with an expectation that their Creator only has the best in mind for His creation that we find rest in the knowledge of His control in our kids' lives. I don't hand my kids over to God (who were never mine to begin with) and think, "Well, I hope it works out!" I am confident that the same Love that worked for me will work for them. Even when it doesn't appear to be "working out" He has the ability to turn it all around. The cool thing is He is not restricted by time. He can capture any heart at any minute.

His love overcame all of my parents' mistakes and short-comings raising me as well as all my mistakes and shortcomings raising my children. I can pray for wisdom and guidance in every step of my parenting. I can pro-actively enforce and instill godly values and character in each of my kids. All this is good and admirable to do. But all confidence is ultimately resting in His hand on our lives. George Barna writes:

> *The scriptures remind us that while we may have free will, we do not posses control over reality. Nothing drives that point home harder than our experiences raising children. Our job is not to succeed but to be obedient to God's calling and principles and allow Him to produce the outcomes according to His perfect will. With that in mind, perhaps we can take a deep breath and relax. As much as you love your children, God loves them more. As deeply as you desire to do what is best for your children, God wants' it even more urgently. As we rely upon Him rather than our own ideas and wisdom, we can be assured that our young ones will experience the best that God has to offer, through us and others.*[6]

We may be compelled as parents to love, protect, instruct, encourage and nurture our children. But there is a *hands down* agreement that the end result in every area of their lives is reliant on the grace and sovereignty of God. Even our own

---

[6] George Barna, *Revolutionary Parenting: What the Research Shows Really Works* (Carol Stream, IL: Tyndale House Publishers, 2007), 16.

ability to love, protect, instruct, encourage and nurture our children is sourced in His grace. We can rest in His love working through us and in His love working through our children.

God in His goodness will always remind me that, even in all my attentiveness as a mother, the outcome of my children's health, safety, spiritual path and natural success is fully in the hands of their Creator. It is in that place that I am aware of the rest and ease He has made for me as a mother. As my children grow, my trust in God grows. Seeing His faithfulness along the way inspires more and more trust within. Without knowing fully that God was in control, the task of parenting would feel impossible.

Parenting is completely easy or completely impossible, depending on who has the reins. Make it easier on yourself. Let go. Trust and believe He is always in control.

Chapter 9
The Practice of Solitude
… and finding 'me' time

It is amazing how one moment of silence can re-center a busy mom. I don't know about you, but my house can be insanely noisy. For me, solitude can come in the simple form of a shower; I get so much clarity in the shower!

After so many years of living with little kids, I have grown accustomed to the hum and clatter of life going on around us. Sometimes I forget just how action-packed my house can be, until someone who isn't often around kids comes over for a visit. The look on the person's face reminds me that *not all humans function under such stimulation*. I remember the first time I was alone at home while someone watched all the kids. I just sat there, for the first hour, in shock at how silent my house can be when I am the only one at home! Engaging my senses in silence has definitely been a coveted commodity in my life.

Time away is valuable as a mother. A place of solitude where you can be alone with your thoughts is very important. Whether it is a peaceful walk on the beach or a just a visit to the bathroom (with a good lock on the door), pulling away is vital to recharging for us parents. The Lord pulled away often in scripture. He also recommended that His disciples escape the business of the day, "Come with me by yourselves to a quiet place and get some rest" (Mark 6:30, NIV).

Oh how I cherish those sweet moments of solitude! If I could package the essence of *quiet time* in such a way that I could market it and sell it to mothers, I would be rich!

When my kids were all really little, babies and toddlers, I would seldom get a chance to pause and hear from God. I was so busy and so tired at the end of the day, I wouldn't even remember hitting my pillow before I was out. It was in that season that I used to have the most lucid and directional dreams. God would come and show me something or refresh me in my sleep. I would wake up knowing Holy Spirit had ministered to me, in such a personal way. It was such a gift to have Him refresh me in the night; it was His grace and goodness giving me what I needed for the next day, all while I slept! If you are that busy mom with babies and toddlers, know that refreshing is available amid the whirlwind ... even if it is right in the middle of your sleep!

If your quiet times seem so few and far between, ask God to multiply the rest and rejuvenation in ways only He can. He knows how challenging it is for you to get away; fortunately, He is not limited by your busy schedule. He lives outside the restraints of time. Somehow He is able to refresh you even in the most burned out stages and seasons of your life. His grace wants to chase you down and lavish you with rest in the middle of it all.

Remembering you
Years ago I had a dream. In this dream I was very sick and did not know it. I went to a doctor, and as he examined me, he pointed out all these obvious physical symptoms and areas of my body that were decaying and unhealthy. I said, "That's funny, I never noticed I was dying. I guess I am too busy taking care of my children."

The doctor in my dream said, "Well, if you don't take time to take care of yourself you will die, and then your children won't have a mom." When I woke up from the dream, I knew that the doctor represented the Father. *Doctor God* was reminding me to take care of myself!

I was really busy with life at that time, and I was very focused on my children, our ministry and the people that were around us. I really needed to pull away and spend time taking care of myself spiritually and naturally. I am so thankful Holy Spirit showed me this.

You are an individual!
Somewhere your children end and you begin. And vice versa. In the midst of serving our family we can easily forget to take care of ourselves. Being a sacrificial mother seems to morph into *martyr mother* syndrome for a lot of us moms. The woman who no longer takes care of herself, does anything for herself and no longer values her needs is not doing her family or her soul any good. Your family needs *you* to take care of yourself. Your need to remain *you* and value your needs is so important.

I believe there is a beautiful balance in the mother that lays down her life for her family and also maintains a sense of individuality. A mother automatically has the calling of a servant, and we know how highly a servant is esteemed in the kingdom. But her servant heart, birthed out of a love for her family, should enhance her individuality and identity, not dismiss who she is.

We may need to lay down a few dreams to raise our children; I obviously won't be off pursuing a career in high fashion modeling in France. But I know it is important to take care of myself, both spiritually and naturally.

It is vital to remember what you like and do not like. It is important to remember what makes you laugh and come alive. Remember who you are and explore the depths of who Christ is within you. Feel free to make new discoveries about yourself as you grow as a woman. You have deep treasures and talents that uniquely make up who you are, separate from, but also alongside your children and husband. Be bold and fearless to explore who you are.

Take care of your physical appearance; don't put on the sweats (at least not every day) and Disney character t-shirts. Get a new haircut for goodness sake. Put some make-up on and dress in something stylish. That is not vain and selfish; it's healthy.

Keep up with realistic hobbies or activities that you love. While you may not have the time to develop your hobbies into full-time careers, still find time to do what interests and inspires you here and there. Your children crave to recognize you as the beautiful, gifted person you are. Every time I dress up for a date with my husband, or paint a new painting, my children's faces light up. Your children need to know who you are. By modeling a strong sense of individuality you will inspire your children to do the same. Looking back, although I am so grateful for my mother's sacrifices, I wish she had taken care of her needs more. My mother had a tendency to live through her children. I know this is because she didn't know her value.

Mothers are some of the strongest people I know. They just keep on truckin'. Being sick or tired or needy doesn't seem to be an option as a mom. To afford a personal day in the middle of all the needs of the family seems like a luxury we cannot afford. But being tuned into yourself and honest with yourself, knowing what you can really handle is so healthy for the whole family's well being. Good boundaries are so important. Being able to say, "Mommy needs to shut the door to my room for a little while for some quiet time," will teach your young child to honor and respect your space and the space of others.

Being honest with your husband about needing a kid break before you have a melt down is something that he needs to be able to receive and something you never need to feel guilty about. My husband quickly learned the benefit of giving me some time to myself, so he is eager to send me off quite often.

I have to make a choice to take care of myself. If there are dishes to be done and I have the option to exercise or do those dishes, sometimes the better choice will be to exercise. If you pick up tacos at the local taqueria for dinner instead of preparing a gourmet meal for the family, just so you have a little more free time to read at the coffee shop, well good for you! Carving out a little time and finding something, even a little something, to refresh and reclaim your energy and inspiration as a person will be a benefit to everyone around you. If you don't have a whole hour, take 20 minutes. If you don't have 20 minutes, then it may be time to reevaluate some schedules. Something may need to give before mom does.

You can do most everything, mom, but you cannot do it all. Motherhood will always require humility. Motherhood will always demand a selfless substance of love. But it is not just about love for our family, but also a love for ourselves. Don't be afraid to love yourself enough to take time and value your needs.

Chapter 10
The Practice of Rest
... and the importance of play

I don't know about you, but I have found myself in way too many frantic and frenzied moments trying to do it all for my children. I want to make as many lasting memories and celebrate all the milestones of childhood. While it is not a bad desire to make plans and do things to make life special for our children, sometimes our efforts and the events on our calendars can overwhelm the family and run us ragged.

I was watching some old, family home videos recently with my oldest daughter, and we came across a video of her first piano recital. All that the camera captured was my sweet little girl playing, "Hark Hear the Bells" in a pretty Christmas dress. I remember that day perfectly. What the camcorder did not capture were the frantic moments leading up to the recital. My husband was gone on a trip, and I had to drag all four of my children to that piano recital. I had a nursing baby to feed and change, a tired toddler who missed her nap, a busy preschooler to contain and my oldest daughter to help prepare and look her best for her big recital. And, as usual, we were running late. It was a mess. It was one of those parenting moments we all wish we could do over. I was sweating and scrambling to get ready and yelling for everyone to pull it together. All those poor little kids were just standing there dependently, not knowing how to help mom out. And my poor oldest daughter ... right before her special performance, all I could do was bark orders at her as she scrambled to prepare and help gather her siblings. When we got to the church late and could not find parking, I could have just cried. It wouldn't have made a difference because all of the kids had cried by that point. We scrambled into the little church and did our best to quietly find a seat. Despite all the chaos, my little eight-year-old girl played beautifully before her audience, and that was the only part captured in our home video. I asked my daughter, as we watched her younger self smiling and playing her song, if she remembered that day. I hoped she had forgotten the horrible way her mother dealt with all the stress leading up to the event. She said, "Yeah, I remember that day all right, it was horrible! You yelled at me and made me cry right before I had to play a difficult piano piece before a group of strangers." While my daughter doesn't hold that memory against me, we both agreed that it would have been better to have *thrown in the piano recital towel* and admitted that bringing four little kids to that particular event, by myself, was not a good idea.

Sometimes we can pull off recitals, bake sales and parties while making sweet memories revolving around these grand events, and sometimes we simply cannot. We have been to Disneyland one year and had the time of our lives, and we have been to Disneyland another year and totally regretted it. It seemed our young family lived moment-to-moment. We learned that being sensitive to the day and pacing our schedules is key. Knowing how to find rest and not neglecting that rest for another activity will save mom some unneeded stress and our children some bad memories.

For my children, less can be more. Quality over quantity, when planning our lives as a family, is important. When reflecting back on my own childhood, some of my fondest memories surround some of the simplest moments because they were peaceful and meaningful. It is funny the things that make up our favorite childhood memories. Whether it was my mom painting my toenails or my dad singing me a funny song before bed, it's clear that what makes up the joyful memories cannot be guaranteed by elaborate efforts.

I have overcomplicated many moments, such as my children's birthdays. Instead of small, meaningful celebrations between a few family members, because we are a celebratory family, we love to throw big complicated parties. Planning a birthday party for one of my children can produce the most stressful day for me. I spend the time getting the cake finished, decorating, making sure my child is presentable; and before I know it the guests are about to arrive and I haven't even showered. I can get so frantic and stressed out that I wonder what the point of the whole production really is. If I am operating from a place of stress and obligation to make a lasting memory, then the joy of something meant to be a wonderful experience can all too quickly evaporate into a meaningless fog. Quality can be replaced by quantity, when all the while our child would have been just as honored by a quiet birthday in the company of their family.

Entering His rest

We all crave and appreciate the value of rest. Rest is what we are searching for. Rest gives our lives substance and quality. No matter how busy or intense parenting becomes for you, when you are completing a task out of a place of rest, there is so much more productivity, and more importantly, joy filling your life with sweet memories and substance.

Rest is the honey and oil of life. Rest is what makes life sweet. Rest is what makes even the hardest moments seem easy. I want to enjoy what I am doing, but it is impossible to do so unless I am in a place of inward peace. Finding that place of peace and rest, where we can step back and really enjoy our family, is where life is good! Without rest, or the *Spirit of Rest,* in our homes, the aspects of life that are meant to be happy can quickly seem tainted.

Reciting the beloved Psalm 23, *The Lord is my Shepherd, I shall not be in want. He makes me to lie down in green pastures ...* When I get to the part that says, *He makes me to lie down in green pastures,* I get this hilarious mental picture of God *making me* lie down. I see Him pushing me over into a luscious green pasture to enjoy some R&R. Our Father is so nurturing to us as a whole person. He desires our body, soul and spirit to sip in His rest. I wish every morning I could smell the sweet fragrance of those green pastures, reminding me that wherever I go, and whatever I do, rest is close by.

Sometimes I forget those *green pastures* are waiting for me as my day unfolds. We all forget. There are more than enough opportunities to engage in the stresses of life. Even the slightest things can distract us from rest. How many times have you been late for an appointment and done something ridiculous, like spill your coffee all over yourself? No matter what, even when you spill that coffee at the most inopportune time, purpose to operate out of His rest. Listen to your body and emotions when you are stressed. I think stress is like a pain receptor God has given us that alerts us to *stop and rest or we are likely to get hurt!*

Take a deep breath. Do one thing at a time. SLOW, DOWN.

> *Therefore, since the promise of entering His rest still stands, let us be careful none of you be found to have fallen short of it* (Heb. 4:11, NIV).

Be careful not to miss His rest; you have an ample supply of it! *Jesus Christ is our Sabbath Rest*. Our Rest is a person to whom we are continually united. Without rest you will surely dry out, burn out and break down. He gave us His Spirit of Rest so we can find a sustenance that will emulate a peaceful, patient and graceful countenance. Even in the most chaotic moments, when you feel the whole world is closing in on you, you are going to be at rest. That rest is true peace. When I am walking in that peace, I am a more productive and efficient person, all while being more pleasant to be around. The world will be attracted to this source of rest that you carry. The tired and weary will migrate to you without any explanation.

The serious business of play
In the middle of engaging in His rest, *play!* Find time to be playful during your day. Surprise your kids with something comically shocking! Grab them by surprise in the middle of

cleaning, or tackle them with the vacuum hose and tickle them until they can't handle it any more. Wake them in the middle of the night to go outside and look at the stars. Even if you don't want to, get in the water and play with your kids instead of watching them on the sideline; or totally shock them and serve them banana splits for dinner! Give your kids permission to be silly as often as possible. Be playful with your spouse too, modeling a relationship that remembers how healthy it is to let loose and have fun. Be silly together as a family. Laugh together. Remind your teenagers how fun and important play is before they slip off into seriousness. There is a stark contrast between the one who is too serious to play and the one who is always game!

Play is often talked about as if it were relief from serious learning. But for children play is serious learning. Play is really the work of childhood. – Fred Rogers

Joy is the serious business of Heaven. – C.S. Lewis

If I were to picture family life portrayed as a theater production, the music that would accompany a happy family scene would be the sound of children playing. Child-like play brings such a healthy rhythm and sound to a home.

How blessed are the people who know the joyful sound! O Lord, they walk in the light of your countenance (Ps. 89:15, NIV).

A friend came to stay with our family recently. She does not have any children, so the shock and intensity of staying in a rather small home with four children set in quickly. Can anyone say, *OVER-STIMULATION?* We are a loud family to say the least, so I would find her outside on the deck regularly, catching some fresh air and a moment of silence. On the evening before my friend was about to fly home, I joined her for a glass of wine and a quiet moment on our deck. I made a quick comment about how I thought she would be happy to be back to her

Chapter 10

quiet home! My friend did not respond with the enthusiastic, *"Yes!"* I expected. In fact, she began to cry. She said, "Lily, I am going to miss the beautiful noises of a full home. There is nothing happier than the noise of your children!"

I realized how much I take all of our pandemonium for granted. There will be a time when John and I will miss all the noise. For now, my friend's words reminded me to cherish the exuberant cries and giggles and play that fill my home. My children's voices are music to my ears – a joyful sound!

Remember that allowing play makes for a healthy life. Play is a healthy priority. I have never regretted joining in play with my children, in fact, I only regret not doing it more.

The serious mom
At times I have found myself obligated to be a serious, responsible and intense mom, as if acting stressed and serious is how a mom should be. This mentality tends to be how society portrays mothers. If I adopt that belief, then I start to feel justified in my stressful attitude. Before I know it, I am manifesting stress, huffing and sighing all around the house, or yelling and barking out orders until everyone is tense and walking on eggshells around mom. Stress can be birthed, not necessarily out of reality, but out of fearful habit. I have to stop and remind myself that I am not *that* mom! I have a choice not to *go there!* Acting like a stressed out, disengaged, serious mom is not our portion in Christ. Rest and play are our portions. Rest and play make up the gift we have in Christ. To miss out on the two is to miss out in the gift of salvation entirely.

Are we bad moms when we are serious? *No!* You have to be serious sometimes, but not all the time. Play becomes the essence of being awesomely awake. Just like a group of children exude enthusiastic life, that same playful energy in us causes us to live vitally charged and alert. Challenge yourself to let go a little more, and then a little bit more. Go ahead and dive in! Indulge yourself in this tangible, refreshing treat of play.

92

Chapter 10

I think that no matter what we are doing, no matter how stressful it may seem, if we purpose to play and remain in a cheerful state of mind, we will eventually not be able to make the distinction between *work* and *play*. I want to be *that* kind of mom!

When he marked out the foundations of the earth, I (Wisdom) was with him as someone he could trust. For me, every day was pure delight as I played in His presence all the time, playing everywhere on His earth, and delighting to be with humankind (Prov. 8:29-32, CJB).

Chapter 11
The Practice of Identity
... and nurturing wholeness

You were in before you were out; you were found before you were lost; you were fixed before you were broken; you were lifted before you fell; you were home before you started.
– Benjamin Dunn

I love the whole process of creating a painting. Going from a blank canvas and arriving at a place of completion is such a great feeling. The process is never the same. Some pieces take hours and undergo multiple phases before I am satisfied and call them complete. Some of my other paintings are quick and spontaneous, finished in an afternoon. Some I overwork and ruin with too much fuss and correction, changing shapes and colors until everything becomes a muddy mess. Knowing when to stop and walk away from a piece of artwork in progress can take almost as much discipline as continuing on and being faithful in every detail in the most tedious piece. There is a real *art* to completion – diligence, patience, perseverance and ease are all needed. To walk away, satisfied with a completed work is blissful as an artist.

Completing a task or a goal feels good. It feels like rest. It feels like perfection.

I thank my God every time I remember you. In all my prayers for all of you, I always pray with joy because of your partnership in the Gospel from the first day until now, being confident of this, that he who began a good work in you will carry it on to completion until the day of Christ Jesus (Phil. 1:3-6, NIV).

A lot of people look to this passage as a pep talk to someone who is feeling defeated or imperfect in themselves, hoping that one day, *in the great by and by*, they will acquire a status of being complete. But what the apostle Paul is really communicating is a reminder that Christ Himself has perfected us in His own death and resurrection – and He is the one who ultimately brings this already existent truth to light. In Him we are already found, even when we feel lost. In Him we already have our completion, even on the days when we don't see our goals manifest, and on the days when we our house feels in turmoil. While we are learning and growing in the revelation of who we are in Him, the fact is we are already foundationally born into His completeness.

How do you see yourself? How do you see your children? Do you know how complete and perfect you are? My prayer and hope for you, as you read these pages, is that your mind will awaken to the truth of who you are, in light of the finished work of the cross, and that you can identify with Christ as the substance and source of who you have become: a new creation in His image. You are a masterpiece! You are His artwork. *Finito!* You are finished!

Identifying with the Gospel
C.S. Lewis said, *"You are what you believe."*

Identity frames up action. We must realize that the Lord has given us a new heart and a new mind. Our mind and thoughts are merely being awakened to the simple fact that He has already perfected them!

> *Do not conform any longer to the pattern of this world, but be transformed by the renewing of your mind. Then you will be able to test and approve what God's will is – His good, pleasing and perfect will* (Rom. 12:2, NIV).

When we are convinced in our mind, when we believe something to be truth, then that is what we will ultimately manifest. The pattern is this: *entertain a thought, the thought becomes what you believe, and your beliefs project actions.* It is not our actions that dictate our identity, but our identity which dictates our actions. We must think, know and believe the truth about ourselves, in order for that truth to bring tangible liberty to our lives: *you will **know** the truth, and the truth will set you free* (John 8:32).

The Gospel, being continually solidified in our minds and adapted as a belief, is destined to manifest our best! The truth – thanks to Jesus – is that we look like Him, whether we know it or not ... but let us meditate on that reality! There is such a need for a makeover in our minds as believers. We will act according to what we believe we are. What you believe about your children will be the identity you speak over them. A parent who is confident to speak true identity over a young life brings so much glory to God.

Throughout the Gospel the story of our completion is illustrated and told through the story of Christ's death. Our old sinful identity was "co-crucified with Him" (Gal. 2:20) In His death we find our completion, and dare we say, our perfection!

Our actions do not dictate our identity – the opposite is true. Even when my children are manifesting less than their potential, the truth of their identity in Christ is still perfection. Truth always supersedes experience, *period.* By bolstering the truth in them that they are a new creation, that they are "holy and blameless in love" (Eph. 1:4), their behavior begins to reflect this reality.

Confidence in the truth
Insecurity is really just a combination of fear and pride. Even if our insecurity is born out of hurt inflicted on us, to feel inadequate and unfit is to think you had the strength on your own to generate worthiness to begin with. To have full confidence in His declaration about who we are enables us to stop striving for perfection on our own. Modeling this confidence is not pride; it is actually modeling true humility. It is believing what He says about us.

Chapter 11

I think of all the ridiculous things I have done or said that have wounded others or myself, and I see how many of my actions stemmed out of a place of insecurity. In fact, pretty much every stupid or selfish thing I have done, I did as a result of a lack of identity and self-worth, *i.e. insecurity*.

For my daughter's ninth birthday, we surprised her with a pet bunny – a little Mini Holland Lop. Our daughter is a major animal lover, so when John came out with a baby bunny secretly tucked in his bathrobe pocket on the morning of her birthday, my daughter was simply undone and beside herself with joy. She actually started to cry. It was simply one of the sweetest moments witnessed in parenting history. She named her bunny *Aurora*.

After the honeymoon and adrenalin of getting acquainted with a sweet new pet started to fade, we realized that we had better learn how to raise this creature properly. We decided to check out as many books from the library on rabbits as possible. We learned about a healthy diet for our bunny, how to groom her and other tips on training her.

One of the most helpful pieces of information we read pertained to handling our rabbit: *Handle your rabbit with confidence. When your rabbit senses you are sure and confident, she will relax and allow you to take charge.* As we experimented with training our bunny, we quickly learned how important being confident with her really was in training and taking care of her. Any time we hesitated or were timid around her, she would get all skittish and dodge us, making it impossible to groom, train or cuddle with her. Now, when we are relaxed and confident, she just senses it and follows our lead.

My children can be like our little bunny. The whole process with our new pet was such a simple example for me in raising and training my children. They respond to my confidence. When I know who I am, they begin to know who they are. When I know who they are in Christ, I am confident to settle for nothing less.

Chapter 11

When we handle our children with ease and assuredness, they will respond. When our homes emulate confidence, our children find a rest and freedom from so many insecurities in the world.

We have a real, tangible confidence to pass on to our children, a confidence in Christ and a confidence in Christ within. When you were given your children, it was no mistake! You have all you need to parent them, even though you doubt yourself at times. You have a constant Helper. When you know this, it is such an inspiration in daily parenting. When you know your completeness, you can't help manifesting the security that your children crave. Completion is your true identity. Completion is the identity your children are designed to grow into.

Single-minded vision

Galatians 2:20 has become a favorite mantra in our home, *"for it is not longer I that live, but Christ lives within me."* This scripture dictates our perspectives regarding our capabilities in every facet of life.

Having the perspective that our old self is dead, and Christ is now made alive in us, is so important for mothers and fathers to understand so that we can pass on this point of view to our kids. How can we begin to infuse the truth of their identity if we are confused about our own? Teaching our children that we have a Savior, who has conquered all that hinders us, is a good reminder for us all to look for Christ within, and refuse to give way to any thing less than a Christ-like life.

People have commented to me that we seem to be "a family that lives a celebratory lifestyle." I rejoice when I hear that, because I know it's true. We are celebrating a victory, even in the middle of the growth, maturation process and challenges we face. If this Gospel is meant to produce anything, it is meant to produce a big, fat, party. Living a celebratory lifestyle should come naturally as a Christ-centered family because the Gospel is worth celebrating. Don't mourn the death of your old nature; celebrate a new life.

Chapter 11

The believer that constantly bounces between completeness and incompleteness is like a homeless man wandering the streets. The mind that wavers between rest and unrest will never feel at home. Be at home with the revelation of your perfection. Be single-minded and confident in your identity in Christ. Your old self doesn't exist. You need not face continual temptation to identify with that false identity. Don't let your mind wander there, vacillating between rest and working on your own salvation. Be stubborn and single-minded in who Christ says you are. Purpose to surround yourself with a community of believers who identify with Christ's victory. Share in the celebration with like-minded people.

Train up a child in the way he should go, and when he is old he will not depart from it (Prov. 22:6, NIV).

Giving our children direction in the way they should go is dependent foremost on telling them *who they already are* in Christ. This is crucial to nurturing their design. In every correction, in guiding our children to better behavior, the underlying reality is to always point them to the new creation reality found in Christ's death for all of us. We can say to a younger child, "Don't hit!" without labeling them as a mean kid. We don't call them "bad kids" when they do bad things. That only bolsters the lie of the false self. Instead, we appeal to the truth of who they are.

"You are a good boy, right? ... Does a good boy hit his brother?"

Remember that behavior and sin management is not your priority, though it may feel that way in the middle of a chaotic day. Your priority is always to bolster the Gospel truth of Christ in them. Amazingly, the more they believe the truth about themselves, the less they act up!

We can remind them that they are nice, kind, gentle and loving, even if they are not manifesting *nice* and *kind*. That is who

Christ created and redeemed them to be. As our children get older and our conversations with them deepen and mature, we still point them to *who* they are as a result of *who* Christ is in them. We can offer them only one path to victory over any character hindrance they may be encountering. We point them in one direction only!

> *I will have handicapped you for life, quite possibly, if I teach you that something outside of yourself is greater than that which is in you.* – Danny Silk[7]

There is only one antidote for our problems and all that keeps us from living a Christ-like life. Once our children identify with *Christ within* they are simply destined for greatness. To see a person confident in their true identity in God is so awesome.

Our desire as parents to instill confidence, a true sense of self-purpose, godly character, and fullness of identity in our children can tempt us to formulate a set of rules. While rules and formulas are not evil within themselves, they becomes toxic when viewed as a means of *achieving* that godly identity. Only the incarnation, death and resurrection of the Son of God was capable of producing true holiness.

It is disorienting and overwhelming for me to filter through all the step-by-step parenting books that I have come across, trying to find something that will work for each of my children. Sometimes I wish there was one single *parenting encyclopedia* that would list every obstacle I ever encountered with each of my kids, alphabetically, followed by the perfect remedy. Jesus is the remedy. He is the plan and formula. He will use and move your heart in the right direction, because from His perspective, He's already given you a new one. Your own efforts are nothing without His hand. Even our ability to trust Him is a gift.

---

[7] Danny Silk, *Loving Our Kids on Purpose* (Shippensburg, PA: Destiny Image Publishers, 2008), 59.

Chapter 11

When we rely on the simplicity of the cross and realize that Christ lives within, we are filled with the right words for our children and loved ones. When we speak over our children we need to remember what our Creator spoke over us when we were lost and broken: *Perfect! Finished!*

Wells of encouragement

When my son was very little, maybe three, we were quietly driving down the road when he broke the silence with the random question, "Are you pleased with me, Mom?"

I remember his sweet little round face and his big brown eyes, so pure and expectant as he asked me his question. "Of course I am pleased with you," I said with no hesitation.

This same little boy, when learning to ride a bike, would freak me out so much because instead of looking in front of him to see where he was going, he would look directly at my face waiting for some sort of approval and excitement in my expression. I would quickly have to yell out, "Good job, son! You are so amazing!" just so he would focus on the road again. Riding the bike was not the main thrill for this little guy, it was also the excitement and approval of a mom that stood by to watch.

It is not just my son that is looking for my approval. I stand by all of my children, looking for every opportunity to give them a big thumbs up!

My children, all children, need to know how pleased we are with them. They are looking for our approval at every age. I am all grown up, and I still personally love to know I have my parents' approval. There is a natural, healthy desire God gives us as children to crave approval from our parents. To grow up not knowing a father or mother's approval can be so debilitating and create so many insecurities.

Chapter 11

Children need to hear you say, *Good job! I am so proud of you! You are lovely, beautiful and perfect!* They need to hear your words of encouragement every day. Whether or not you have the *natural gift* of encouragement, if you have been given kids, you better lavish them with meaningful praise!

Your words of encouragement solidify a deep sense of worth and unconditional love within your children that they will carry with them well into their adulthood. Compliment them on everything you love about them. If you need to correct and criticize behavior, precede and follow up with encouragement. Always let your children fall asleep with the peace of a mother's approval. Whether *new age* or Christian, Marianne Williamson states a truth that is universally human in her famous quote:

> *Our deepest fear is not that we are inadequate. Our deepest fear is that we are powerful beyond measure. We ask ourselves, "Who am I to be brilliant, gorgeous, talented and fabulous?" Actually, who are you not to be? We were born to make manifest the glory of God that is within us. And as we let our own light shine, we unconsciously give other people permission to do the same.*

About the Author

Lily Crowder is a mother of four and lives in Portland, Ore. with her husband, John. The Crowders minister internationally as authors, speakers and advocates of supernatural Christianity. They are on the forefront of a fresh renewal movement marked by the message of grace, ecstatic experience, miracles and a recovery of the foundational preaching of the finished work of the cross. As founders of Sons of Thunder Ministries and Publications, they speak at schools and conference events around the world. SOT hosts mass evangelism events and operates multiple homes for orphan children in developing nations. They have a background in church planting and currently oversee *Cana New Wine Seminary* in Portland. Along with their bi-annual magazine, *The Ecstatic*, SOT also produces a weekly video teaching, *The Jesus Trip,* which has garnered more than a million views. John and Lily have a heart to see the Kingdom of God manifest creatively in every sector of society. Their vision is to equip the Church and reach the world by clearly communicating the finished work of the cross. Creative miracles and unusual signs and wonders mark their ministry.

Connect With Us

SONSOFTHUNDER

There are many ways to stay connected with us!

Visit us online at:
www.TheNewMystics.Com

Find out about conferences, mission trips, schools, teaching resources, our itinerary and more.

Email us at:
info@thenewmystics.org

Write us at:
P.O. Box 40
Marylhurst, OR 97036

Call us toll-free:
1-877-343-3245

Find us on Social Networks:
Facebook:
www.facebook.com/lilycrowder
www.facebook.com/revjohncrowder
Twitter: www.twitter.com/thenewmystics
YouTube: www.youtube.com/sonsofthunderpub
Linkedin: www.linkedin.com/in/johnwcrowder
We are also on Google +

Monthly Web Conference

Discover our live monthly Web seminar: *The Inner Sanctum*

THENEWMYSTICS.TV

The Inner Sanctum continues to be a fun connection point for Gospel drinkers all around the globe who want to stay plugged in with finished-work theology in an atmosphere of joy and impartation. Members now have access to dozens of hours of archived shows, making it the most comprehensive place to view Sons of Thunder teachings. And each month, the Crowders and guests engage one-on-one with viewers for live teaching and Q&A sessions.

Our Inner Sanctum Web broadcast provides a user-friendly format and we continue to add more interactive features. The Inner Sanctum is also a social media platform where members create a personal profile, share pictures and chat with friends 24-hours a day, even when the show is not live.

Find out about membership for yourself, your church or a home group by visiting **www.TheNewMystics.TV**

The Ecstatic Magazine

We produce our bi-annual magazine *The Ecstatic* as a way to bring a cohesive voice to the growing interest in authentic, mystical Christianity – a mysticism rooted in the grace message of Christ's cross – not in dead works, asceticism or external disciplines. In a practical sense, *The Ecstatic* serves as an information gateway to the ministry of John & Lily Crowder. But moreover, it is a first fruit in publishing toward bridging several important themes that are converging at the moment: finished work theology, the miraculous, divine satisfaction and daily human existence in the incarnational life. All of these concepts are intrinsically woven together with contributions from modern writers and ancient voices. A new grace-based, Christ-centered mysticism is on the rise. It is bridging many streams. Relevant is its cultural approach. Radical is its Charismatic fervor. Reformative is its theology of grace. These are guiding values of this publication and our own lives. It is a theological journal whose frequency is joy unspeakable.

Subscribe to John Crowder's magazine, *The Ecstatic,* with any donation: **www.TheNewMystics.com/Ecstatic**

Digital Download Store

Visit our online *Digital Download Store* to get instant audio teachings on many topics from the Crowders at: **www.JohnCrowder.Net**

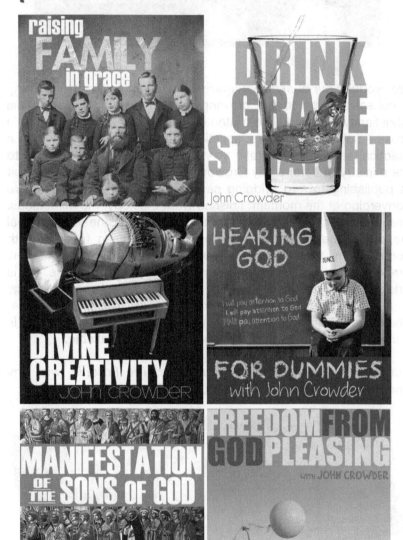

More Books from Sons of Thunder

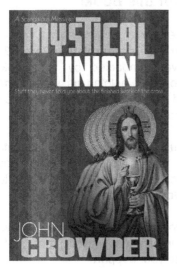

Mystical Union
A Scandalous Message!
When you think of the cross, do you think of *fun*? Get ready for the Gospel as you've never heard it. With clear revelatory truths on the New Creation and the scandalous joys of the cross, Mystical Union is one of John's most revolutionary, life-changing works. The happy Gospel of grace is about uninterrupted union with the Divine. This book lays out our most core beliefs. It promises to wreck your theology and cheer you up with undeniable Biblical truths on the free gift of perfection.
$19.95 + Shipping (Hardback)

The Ecstasy of Loving God
Trances, raptures & the supernatural pleasures of Jesus Christ
God has destined you to live in the joyful radiance of Himself, just as Adam was called to live in the realm of Eden. Ecstasy, or "extasis," is the Greek term for trance, and is linked with a pleasurable, God-given state of out-of body experience recorded throughout the sciptures and the Church age. In this book, John takes us on a journey from past to present to introduce us to a lifestyle of a deep practice of God's presence. **$20 + Shipping**

**FIND MORE AT WWW.THENEWMYSTICS.COM/BOOKS
OR CALL TOLL-FREE 1-877-343-3245**

Our Newest Releases

Order More Copies of this Book!

Did you enjoy ...
Grace for the Contemplative Parent?
If you were impacted by this book, please consider helping us spread the word and share the glorious revelation of grace to other parents!

Contact us about bulk order discounts for your friends, church, Bible study groups or even pass it out as a gift to local pastors in your region.

For multiple, bulk order copies, contact us at info@thenewmystics.org. We appreciate your support!

A Brand New Release From John Crowder ...

Cosmos Reborn
Take a grace-centered look at regeneration, the new creation and the new birth. Christ cured the human condition. John's new book explores the universal scope of the cross - if one died for all, then all died! "For God was in Christ reconciling the cosmos to Himself." He has woven humanity into His divinity! Dispel the myth of a dark, schizophrenic god of religion. This book makes a scandalous case that the Father of Jesus Christ is in a good mood. Get a religious detox – a dose of happy theology – liberating good news!

$19.95 +Shipping only at **www.thenewmystics.com**

Cana Seminary

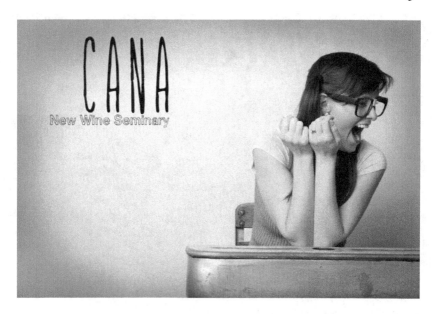

Cana is where the water of the word is transformed into the wine of contemplative experience. Students, pastors and lay leaders who want a grace immersion are invited to join us for a summer of intensive theological training and hands on impartation in an atmosphere of joy unspeakable in Portland, Oregon.

The Crowders host this unique three-month seminary for wild-eyed wonder junkies to be deeply established in the revelation of the Gospel of grace. Cana offers a unique marriage of life-transforming, happy theology woven seamlessly with an intoxicating practice of the presence of God. Where else will you find doctorate level theologians and mystical ecstatics on the same platform? Cana is a drunken seminary. A three-month theological circus of fun geared to saturate students with the Living Word - in the wine of the New Covenant. More than a ministry school ... Cana is a *Message School*.

www.Cana.Co

Partner with us!